CAMBRIDGE ENGLISH for schools
Student's Book Two

ANDREW LITTLEJOHN & DIANA HICKS

PUBLISHED BY THE PRESS PYNDICATE OF THE UNIVERSITY OF CAMBRIDGE
The Pitt Building, Trumpington Street, Cambridge CB2 1RP, United Kingdom

CAMBRIDGE UNIVERSITY PRESS
The Edinburgh Building, Cambridge CB2 2RU, United Kingdom
40 West 20th Street, New York, NY 10011-4211, USA
10 Stamford Road, Oakleigh, Melbourne 3166, Australia

© Cambridge University Press 1996

This book is in copyright. Subject to statutory exception
and to the provisions of relevant collective licensing agreements,
no reproduction of any part may take place without
the written permission of Cambridge University Press.

First published 1996
Fourth printing 1998

Printed in Italy by G. Canale & C. S.p.A. - Borgaro T.se (Turin)

ISBN 0 521 42170 5 Student's Book
ISBN 0 521 42174 8 Workbook
ISBN 0 521 42178 0 Teacher's Book
ISBN 0 521 42182 9 Class Cassette Set
ISBN 0 521 42131 4 Workbook Cassette

Contents

Map of *Cambridge English for Schools 2* 4
What's in *Cambridge English for Schools 2?* 8

1 Welcome back! 10
2 TEST YOUR ENGLISH The world encyclopaedia 13
    EXTENSION The world encyclopaedia 16

THEME

A A good life
3 TOPIC Sports for everybody 24
4 LANGUAGE FOCUS 30
5 ACTIVITY A good life 36
6 CULTURE MATTERS At school in the United States 38
7 REVISION AND EVALUATION 40

B Life on Earth
8 TOPIC In a rainforest 44
9 LANGUAGE FOCUS 50
10 ACTIVITY Poems from the rainforest 56
11 CULTURE MATTERS Discover America! 58
12 REVISION AND EVALUATION 60

C Back in time
13 TOPIC Detectives of history 64
14 LANGUAGE FOCUS 70
15 ACTIVITY Discoveries for the future 76
16 CULTURE MATTERS The history of the USA 78
17 REVISION AND EVALUATION 80

D Below the clouds
18 TOPIC Climates of the world 84
19 LANGUAGE FOCUS 90
20 ACTIVITY A new book of world climates 96
21 CULTURE MATTERS An outdoor life 98
22 REVISION AND EVALUATION 100

E Across borders
23 TOPIC The global village 104
24 LANGUAGE FOCUS 110
25 ACTIVITY Come to see us! 116
26 CULTURE MATTERS Britain is an island 118
27 REVISION AND EVALUATION 120

F Energy in our lives
28 TOPIC Blackout! 124
29 LANGUAGE FOCUS 130
30 ACTIVITY Save your energy! 136
31 CULTURE MATTERS Energy at home 138
32 REVISION AND EVALUATION 140

THEME TRAIL A revision game 143
SUPPLEMENTARY UNIT A A Parcel of English 146
SUPPLEMENTARY UNIT B Making an Exercise Box 148
Irregular verbs 149
Ideas list 150
Map of the world 152
Songs 154
Wordlist/Index 156

Map of Cambridge English for Schools 2

	UNIT	UNIT
Curriculum links: *Geography* - life in various countries; *Biology* - lives of animals; *Science* - space.	**1 Welcome Back!** 10 The people in your class; things to help you learn; general world knowledge; a tour of the book.	**2 TEST YOUR ENGLISH** 13 **The world encyclopaedia** A test covering Present simple; pronouns; adjectives; comparatives/superlatives; Past simple.

THEME	TOPIC	LANGUAGE FOCUS
A A good life **Curriculum links:** *Health Education* - sports; types and function of exercise; *Cultural Studies* - school in the United States; *Social Education* - social well-being.	**3 TOPIC Sports for everybody** 24 Sports and health; types of exercise. *Vocabulary areas:* names of sports; parts of the body; daily routines.	**4 LANGUAGE FOCUS** 30 verbs + '-ing'; adverbs; expressing likes and dislikes. *Out and about:* classroom phrases; asking for help.
B Life on Earth **Curriculum links:** *Environmental Science* - importance of trees and rain; *Natural History* - trees, dinosaurs; *Cultural Studies* - natural history in the USA; *Language* - writing poems.	**8 TOPIC In a rainforest** 44 The importance of rainforests; how they make rain and oxygen; the oldest living things. *Vocabulary areas:* places; plants and animals; natural processes.	**9 LANGUAGE FOCUS** 50 Dinosaurs: how they lived; Past simple with regular verbs; 'was' and 'were'. *Out and about:* inviting and suggesting.
C Back in time **Curriculum links:** *History* - using historical clues to learn about the past; life 4,000 years ago; *Cultural Studies* - important events in the history of the United States.	**13 TOPIC Detectives of history** 64 Important inventions and discoveries; the 'Iceman' discovery; using clues from history. *Vocabulary areas:* inventions; tools and discoveries; basic verbs.	**14 LANGUAGE FOCUS** 70 Village life in the past; Past simple: regular and irregular verbs; negatives and questions. *Out and about:* reacting to what people say.
D Below the clouds **Curriculum links:** *Geography* - countries and climate types; *Social Studies* - climate and the way we live; *Cultural Studies* - leisure activities.	**18 TOPIC Climates of the world** 84 Climate and how we live; natural disasters. *Vocabulary areas:* weather and weather effects; seasons; climate types.	**19 LANGUAGE FOCUS** 90 Helping the environment; 'going to'; 'have to'; making plans. *Out and about:* in a café.
E Across borders **Curriculum links:** *Geography* - countries and raw materials; *Economics* - international trade; *Cultural Studies* - connections with other countries.	**23 TOPIC The global village** 104 Trade around the world; what things are made of; raw materials and manufactures. *Vocabulary areas:* countries and continents; raw materials; trade.	**24 LANGUAGE FOCUS** 110 'enough'; 'could' in requests; 'would' in offers. *Out and about:* prepositions of place; asking the way (1).
F Energy in our lives **Curriculum links:** *Science* - how electricity is made, static electricity; *Social Studies* - the importance of electricity; safety; energy use; *Cultural Studies* - energy in the home.	**28 TOPIC Blackout!** 124 Energy and the use of electricity in our lives; the New York blackout; experiments with static electricity. *Vocabulary areas:* basic verbs; safety; electricity.	**29 LANGUAGE FOCUS** 130 Past continuous: imperatives. *Out and about:* asking the way (2).

THEME TRAIL		
SUPPLEMENTARY UNIT A	**A revision game** A game to revise the *Topic* and *Language focus* Units.	143
SUPPLEMENTARY UNIT B	**A Parcel of English** Work in English to send to another country.	146
	Making an Exercise Box Writing your own exercises and using the *Ideas list*.	148

UNIT	UNIT	UNIT
EXTENSION 16 **The world encyclopaedia** *The world of people and places*; adjectives; Present simple. *The world of nature*: Present simple question forms; pronouns. *The world of science*: Present continuous; comparatives and superlatives.		
ACTIVITY	CULTURE MATTERS	REVISION AND EVALUATION
5 ACTIVITY 36 **A good life** Making a poster of your ideas about what 'a good life' is.	**6 CULTURE MATTERS** 38 **At school in the USA** The school day in the United States; timetables and rules.	**7 REVISION AND EVALUATION** 40 Self-assessment. *Revision*: sports; daily routines; likes/dislikes; adverbs; new words. *Evaluation*: discussion of Units 3–6; learning vocabulary. *Open plan*.
10 ACTIVITY 56 **Poems from the rainforest** Writing your own poems; listening to music and sounds from a rainforest.	**11 CULTURE MATTERS** 58 **Discover America!** Natural history in the United States of America; things to see and do there.	**12 REVISION AND EVALUATION** 60 Self-assessment. *Revision*: make your own test. *Evaluation*: discussion of Units 8–11; learning to write. *Open plan*.
15 ACTIVITY 76 **Discoveries for the future** Making a booklet for future generations.	**16 CULTURE MATTERS** 78 **The history of the USA** Important events in United States history; sounds from America's history.	**17 REVISION AND EVALUATION** 80 Self-assessment. *Revision*: new words; Past simple; reacting. *Evaluation*: discussion of Units 13–16; learning pronunciation. *Open plan*.
20 ACTIVITY 96 **A new book of world climates** Making a book cover.	**21 CULTURE MATTERS** 98 **An outdoor life** Leisure activities in the UK and in your country.	**22 REVISION AND EVALUATION** 100 Self-assessment. *Revision*: make your own test. *Evaluation*: discussion of Units 18–21; learning English grammar. *Open plan*.
25 ACTIVITY 116 **Come to see us!** Making a tourist leaflet about your area.	**26 CULTURE MATTERS** 118 **Britain was an island!** Britain and the Channel; the Channel Tunnel.	**27 REVISION AND EVALUATION** 120 Self-assessment. *Revision*: requests; offers; 'enough'; new words; asking the way. *Evaluation*: discussion of Units 23–26; using a dictionary. *Open plan*.
30 ACTIVITY 136 **Save your energy!** Your own invention for saving energy!	**31 CULTURE MATTERS** 138 **Energy at home** Homes in Britain and in your country; energy at home; 'typical' rooms.	**32 REVISION AND EVALUATION** 140 Self-assessment. *Revision*: make a test. *Evaluation*: discussion of Units 28–31; learning to be fluent; a letter to the authors. *Open plan*.

Unit ☐

Unit ☐

Supplementary Unit ☐

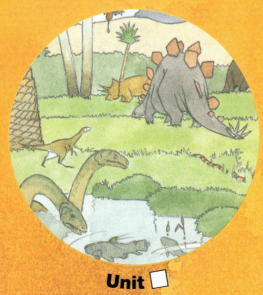

Unit ☐

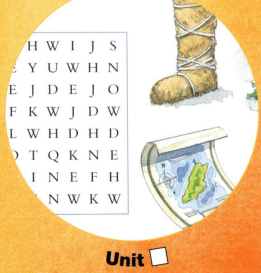

Unit ☐

Welcome to CAMBRIDGE ENGLISH for schools
Student's Book Two

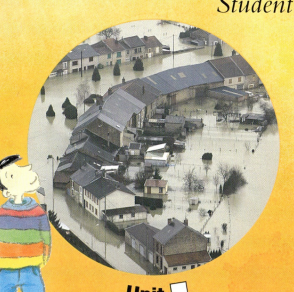

Unit ☐

Unit ☐

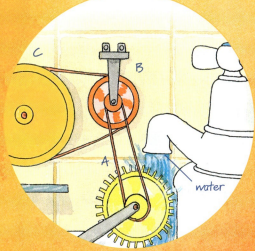

Unit ☐

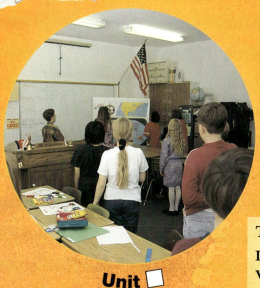

Unit ☐

Take a look at *Cambridge English for Schools 2*
Look through this book. Where can you find the pictures?
Write the Unit number beside each picture.

What's in Cambridge English for Schools 2?

Cambridge English for Schools 2 has three parts for you, the student. There is a Student's Book, a Workbook and a Workbook Cassette.

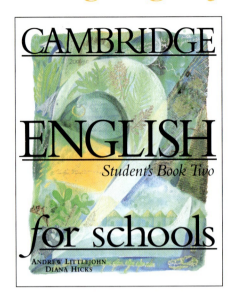
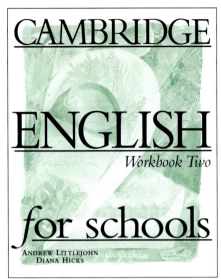
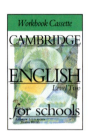

Let's look at the Student's Book

1 The Themes

Match the letter to the name of the Theme. Match the Theme to what you can learn about.

		In it you can learn English and about:
Theme **A** is called …	• Below the clouds	• sports, health and school life
Theme **B** is called …	• Energy in our lives	• climate and life in other countries
Theme **C** is called …	• Across borders	• trade between countries
Theme **D** is called …	• A good life	• energy at home and electricity
Theme **E** is called …	• Back in time	• nature, trees, and dinosaurs
Theme **F** is called …	• Life on Earth	• life thousands of years ago

2 The Units

Read the clues, look at the Units and complete the puzzle.

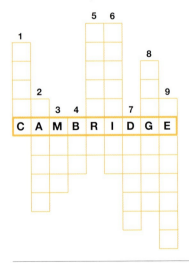

1 Units 3, 8, 13, 18, 23 and 28 are all .... Units.
2 In *Supplementary Unit A* you can make a .... of English to send to another class.
3 There are lots of things to .... in your book. For example, on page 84, you can .... a barometer.
4 You can also make your own exercises and put them in a .... See *Supplementary Unit B*.
5 You can learn about life in the USA and in the UK in .... *matters* Units.
6 Units 5, 10, 15, 20, 25 and 30 are all .... Units. Here you can make or do something with English.
7 There are lots of chances for YOU to .... See, for example, Exercise 5 in Unit 3.
8 Units 4, 9, 14, 19, 24 and 29 focus on ....
9 At the end of every Theme, there is a chance for .... See Units 7, 12, 17, 22, 27, and 32.

3 At the back

Look at pages 149–160. Which pages can
a help you to find a word or topic in the book? Pages ...... to ......
b give you information about the world? Pages ...... to ......
c give you ideas for exercises? Pages ...... to ......
d help with verbs? Page ......

Let's look at the Workbook

4 Inside the Workbook

Look in the Workbook.
Find: a listening exercise
 a writing exercise
 a reading exercise
 a speaking exercise

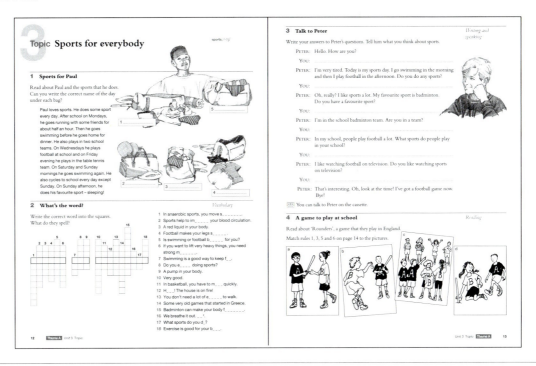

5 The Workbook Units

The Workbook also has six Themes. There are five Units in each one.
What are Units 6, 11, 16, 21, 26 and 31?

6 At the back

Look at the back of the Workbook. What is there?

Let's listen to the Workbook Cassette

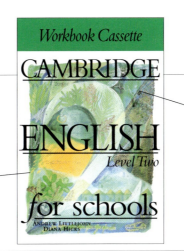

On the cassette, you can find the Workbook exercises.

You can find the songs from the Student's Book.

7 Listen to the page numbers

The cassette tells you the page number for the Units and the Exercises.
Listen. Find the Unit in the Student's Book or Workbook. Write your answers.

a Student's Book page .... is Unit ....
b Student's Book page .... is Unit ....
c Workbook page .... is Unit ....
d .... page .... is ....
e .... page .... is ....
f .... page .... is ....

1 Welcome back!

The people in your class; things to help you learn; a tour of the book

1 What's new?

Discussion and writing
Extra practice • WB Ex. 1, 5

In a small group, tell each other about something that's new in your life.

- We moved to a new house last week.
- I've got a new baby brother.
- I can play the piano and the guitar very well now.
- I've got a new computer.

My name's David. I love football. This year, I am playing for the school team. In the holiday I went to the country. I stayed with my grandfather and grandmother. I went fishing every day.

My name's Susan. I can play the piano and the guitar. I've got a new baby brother. His name is Vincent. He's very beautiful but he cries a lot.

On a small piece of paper, write a few sentences about yourself. Read your papers out to the class or stick them on a plan of your classroom.

2 What do you know?

A puzzle
Extra practice • WB Exs. 2–4

What do you know about the world?
Read the clues and write the correct words in the puzzle.

1 The capital of Japan.
2 The sun is very ....
3 A fly is a type of ....
4 A mammal that gives us milk.
5 England is in the continent of ....
6 Our nearest planet.
7 A flower is a type of ....
8 Three days before Thursday.
9 Paper is made from ....
10 A long river in Egypt.
11 Many years ago people lived in ..... .
12 The smallest planet.
13 .... air falls.
14 The capital of France.
15 Warm .... rises.
16 An insect has six ....
17 The tarantula is a type of ....
18 The parrot is a type of ....
19 A country in South America.

THE WORLD ENCYCLOPAEDIA

10 Unit 1 Welcome back!

3 What can you tell us?

Writing

Work in a small group. Look at these pictures.
Choose two or three and write a part of the world encyclopaedia.

Help each other with words, spellings and grammar.

Ask your teacher to look at what you have written.
Read your work out to the class.

1 The world of people and places

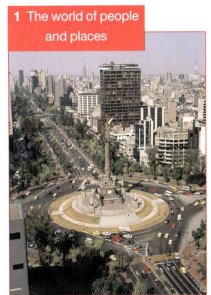

Mexico City: the biggest city in the world

This is Mexico City, the capital of Mexico. It is one of the biggest cities in the world. About 20 million people live there. They speak Spanish in Mexico, and many other Indian languages.

London – the capital of the United Kingdom

Food – to keep us healthy, help us grow and make us strong

2 The world of science

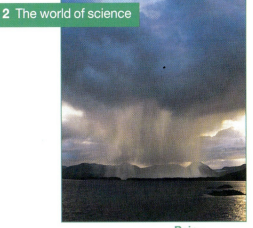

Rain – where does it come from?

The moon – our nearest neighbour

3 The world of nature

Elephants – the largest mammals

The Praying Mantid – beautiful but dangerous

4 The world of history

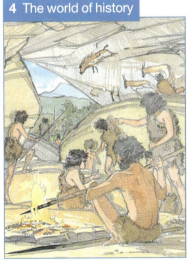

Cavepeople – how they lived and what they did

Dinosaurs – the largest animals on earth

Unit 1 Welcome back!   11

4 Sing a song! All around the world

🔊 Listen to 'All around the world' and sing it with your class. The words are on page 154.

5 Are you ready?

Things to help you learn English

5.1 Some useful things

You can help yourself to learn English.
Here are some things that are very useful.
Talk to your neighbour.
What can you do with each of the things in the picture?
How many of them have you got?

Tell the class your ideas. What other things do you use to help you learn?

5.2 Some useful phrases

You can also help yourself if you ask the right questions!
How do you say these sentences in your language?

- How do you pronounce this word?
- Can you explain that again, please?
- What does ... mean?
- How do you spell ...?
- How do you say ... in English?

6 Find out about your book!

A tour of the book

🔊 Work in a small group. Look at pages 8–9 and do the exercises there.

2 Test your English — The world encyclopaedia

A test covering: social language; Present simple and continuous; adjectives; comparatives; Past simple

Find out how much English you know and learn about people, places, nature and science with the world encyclopaedia!

The world of people and places

1 What are they saying?   *Social language*

Circle the correct answer.

For example:

- (a) How much are these?
- b What size are these?
- c What colour is this?

1
- a What time is it?
- b Is it cold?
- c Do you want one?

2
- a I think they're horrible.
- b I can see them.
- c How many are there?

3
- a How far is the bus station?
- b What time is the bus?
- c Who is the bus driver?

2 Two Mexicos   *Present simple*

Look at these pictures of Mexico. Are the sentences about picture A, or picture B? Circle the answer.

1 There aren't any tall buildings.   A   B
2 The people don't have any cars.   A   B
3 The people live in modern houses.   A   B

Unit 2 Test your English   13

3 Skiing in Switzerland

Adjectives

Circle the correct word.

1 The mountains in Switzerland are very ....
   a dead b high c cheap

2 Many people like skiing there. They think it is very ....
   a tall b ugly c exciting

3 Skiing is sometimes ...., especially if you are going fast.
   a dangerous b friendly c rainy

The world of nature

4 The fantastic world of butterflies

Present tense questions

Read the text and write questions with the question words.

For example: How many …?

How many kinds of butterfly are there?

1 When .... ?

2 Where .... ?

3 How long .... ?

Butterflies

There are about 20,000 different kinds of butterfly. They are easy to see because they have very bright colours. They fly during the day and sleep at night. They live where they can find plants to eat. They do a useful job. They carry the powder – the pollen – which plants make and exchange to grow more plants. Butterflies have a very short life. They usually live for only a few weeks.

5 Animals talk!

Pronouns

Circle the correct pronoun.

1 .... are not the only animals who communicate.
   a Him b Us c We

2 Other animals communicate in different ways. For example, baby birds open .... mouths to show that they are hungry.
   a our b them c their

3 The face of a chimpanzee shows .... feelings.
   a their b your c its

The world of science

6 Make a telephone!

Present continuous

What are they doing?
Write the correct form of the verb to describe the picture.
For example:

(hold) *He is holding the tin.*

1 (make) She .... a hole in the tin.

2 (put) They .... the string in the tins.

3 (talk) He .... to his friend and she can hear him.

7 Facts about the planets

Comparatives and superlatives

Circle the correct answer.

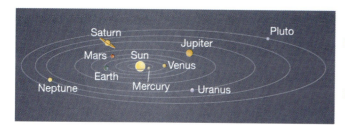

1 Pluto is .... planet.
  a cold   b colder   c the coldest

2 A year on Pluto is .... than a year on Earth.
  a long   b longer   c the longest

3 Mercury is .... planet to the sun.
  a near   b nearer   c the nearest

The world of history

8 Machu Picchu: the lost city of the Incas

Past simple

Circle the correct answer.

1 The Inca people .... in Peru four hundred years ago.
  a live   b lived   c lives

2 Machu Picchu was an Inca city. It .... into the jungle for 350 years.
  a disappear   b is disappearing   c disappeared

3 In 1911 an American explorer, Hiram Bingham, ... Machu Picchu.
  a is finding   b find   c found

4 He .... he was lost in the jungle.
  a thought   b thinks   c is thinking

5 When he travelled back to America, everyone asked him ....
  a 'What do you see?'   b 'What did you see?'   c 'What are you seeing?'

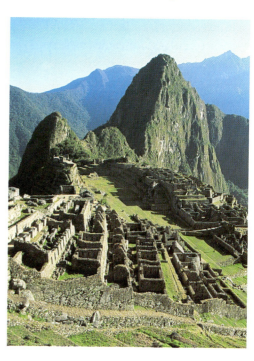

**Look back at the test. Where did you make mistakes?
The extension section gives you more practice.
Choose the parts that you need to do.**

Extension The world encyclopaedia

Look back at your test. Where did you make mistakes?
This extension gives you more practice. Choose the parts you need to do.

The world of people and places

1 In the sun

Look at this picture. How can you describe it?
Put the adjectives under the right heading.

> boring   cold   dry   empty   exciting   expensive   happy   horrible   hot
> nice   dusty   rainy   sunny   ugly   weak   windy   beautiful   dead   friendly

Words that describe the picture	Words that don't describe the picture
hot	rainy

Compare your lists with other students in your class.

Do you like this place? Do you think it is nice to live there?
What do you think people do there?

Adjectives
Extra practice • WB Ex. 1
Extra practice •
TB Ws. 2.1

2 Under the ground

Extra practice • WB Ex. 2
Extra practice •
TB Ws. 2.1

Coober is a town in Australia. You can see a picture of Coober in Exercise 1.
Thousands of people live there. But where are they? Read and find out.

LIFE UNDERGROUND

Coober is a town in Australia. It has schools, banks, shops and sports centres. It has doctors, dentists, teachers and other things you find in a town. It has water, electricity, telephones and television. But it doesn't have many other things. It doesn't have roads. It doesn't have any cars, buses or taxis. It doesn't have any trees or gardens. Coober is completely underground.

It is very hot, dry and dusty near Coober. At night, it is very cold, but in the day it is about 50°C. Because of this, everybody in Coober lives underground. Thousands of people live and work there. Many people work in the opal mines. Their 'houses' are caves.

Pat Watts comes from England but she lives in Coober now. She likes it a lot. She is a dentist there. Her husband works in one of the underground restaurants. 'It's a good place to live,' she says. 'I play tennis every day after work, for example. I don't want to go back to England!'

Do you think Coober is a nice place to live?
Why? Why not? Would you like to live there?

3 Possible or impossible?

Are these things possible or impossible? Write a sentence about each one.

1. Pat's husband goes to work on a bus.
   Impossible! Coober doesn't have any buses.
2. Pat buys her food in a supermarket.
   Possible! Coober has ...
3. Pat's children go to a school in Coober.
4. Pat's children play in the park in Coober.
5. Pat wants to stay in Coober.
6. Pat likes to sit in her garden.
7. The traffic is very bad in Coober.
8. It rains a lot in Coober.

Present simple
Extra practice • WB Ex. 3
Extra practice •
TB Ws. 2.1

4 Your Language Record

Now complete your *Language Record* on page 22.

The world of nature

1 Animal factfile: the leopard

Leopards are very beautiful animals, but how much do you know about them? What questions can you ask? Make a list.

1. Where ...?
2. What ...?
3. How long ...?
4. Why ...?
5. How many ...?

Present tense questions
Extra practice •
WB Ex. 4,5
Extra practice •
TB Ws. 2.2

2 Read about the leopard

How many of your questions can you now answer?

Leopards live in many parts of the world, from Siberia to Africa. They have a very beautiful yellow skin with large black spots. They live for about 15 years and eat small mammals such as young zebras, monkeys, and antelopes. They sleep for about 12 hours a day. Leopards are very solitary animals. They spend most of their time alone in trees, where they wait until a small animal passes. They jump on the animal and then drag it up into the tree, where they eat it.

Like many animals, leopards are disappearing because people hunt them. They kill them for their beautiful coats. The Sinai Leopard, for example, from Egypt, is now probably extinct.

Reading
Extra practice •
WB Ex. 6
Extra practice •
TB Ws. 2.2

 You can listen to the text on the cassette.

3 More animal facts

Making questions

Can you complete these questions and join them to the correct answer?

Which ...*is*... the largest animal in the world?
1 What .... elephants eat?
2 Why .... birds fly south in the winter?
3 How much .... an adult elephant eat in a day?
4 Where .... leopards live?
5 How .... bats know where they are going?
6 How fast .... a cheetah run?

They live in Siberia and Africa.
They send out a sound and wait for the echo.
Up to about 100 km per hour.
About 136 kg of plants.
The blue whale. It's about 25 m long.
They eat fruit, leaves and grass.
Because it's too far to walk!

4 Your own questions

Now work with your neighbour. Think of some questions about the animal world to ask other students in your class. You can look at these pictures for ideas.

Blue whale

Bat

Kangaroo   Tarantula

Cheetah

Collect your questions together.
See how many answers you can find during the next week!

5 Summary

Question forms: a summary

With 'be' and 'can', you make questions by putting the verb before the subject.

	verb	*subject*
Which	is	the largest animal in the world?
How fast	can	cheetahs run?

With most other verbs, you use 'do' or 'does' and the infinitive of the verb.

	do/does	*+ subject*	*+ infinitive*
Why	do	birds	fly south in the winter?
Where	do	leopards	live?
How much	does	an elephant	eat?

Think of some questions about the animal world.
Divide them into columns like the questions above.

6 What's the word?

Pronouns
Extra practice • WB Ex. 7
Extra practice •
TB Ws. 2.2

Choose the correct pronoun for each space.

1 Frogs are reptiles. .... skin is very thick. .... lay eggs. .... blood is cold. (they/them/their)
2 A cow gives milk to .... young. (it/its)
3 We are mammals. .... blood is warm and we give milk to .... babies. (we/our/us)
4 Insects have six legs. Most of .... have wings and can fly. (them/their)
5 Do you like spiders? No! I hate ....! (they/them/their)
6 This is my new dog. Do you like ....? (he/him/his)

Check your answers with your teacher.

7 Your Language Record

Now complete your *Language Record* on page 22.

The world of science

1 Are we alone in the universe?

Discussion

Every year, thousands of people say that they see strange lights in the sky. Many people think that these lights are spaceships – 'flying saucers' – from other planets.

What do you think? Is there life on other planets?
Are we alone in the universe? Do spaceships come to Earth?
How can we find out if there is life on other planets?

Unit 2 Extension

2 How can we find out?

Reading

Scientists are trying to discover if there is life on other planets.
Read about what they are doing. How many things can you count?

IS THERE LIFE ON OTHER PLANETS?

The idea that there is life on other planets is a very old one. In 1959, the United States began to search for life in space and in 1989 a new project started. From the Ames Space Station in California, scientists are now sending radio messages into space every few hours. They want to tell the universe that there is life on Earth. Is anybody listening out there? We really don't know. At the same time, scientists are 'listening' to the radio signals that come to Earth. They are looking for signs of intelligent life on other planets.

Scientists are building very powerful radio telescopes so that they can learn more about the stars and planets. They also hope to learn something from the spaceships. At this moment, spaceships are travelling into space. They are sending photographs back to Earth. Perhaps we can learn a lot from the photographs.

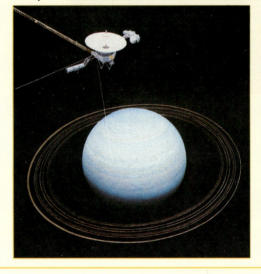

 You can listen to the text on the cassette.

3 They are sending radio messages into space

Present continuous
Extra practice • WB Ex. 8
Extra practice •
TB Ws. 2.3

Look back at the text in Exercise 2. Can you find more examples of sentences like the ones below? They all use 'be' + '-ing'.

  Scientists are sending radio messages into space.
  Is anybody listening out there?

The sentences all contain examples of the Present continuous tense.
Do you remember when we use the Present continuous?

What is the difference between these sentences?

  He's opening the door.   He opens the door every morning at 9.00 am.
  She's writing a letter to her mother. She writes a letter to her mother every week.

4 What's happening?

Look at these pictures. What is happening in each one? Write ten sentences.

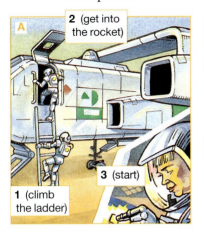
A
1 (climb the ladder)
2 (get into the rocket)
3 (start)

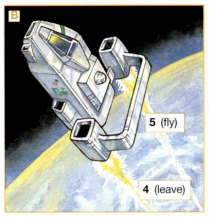
B
4 (leave)
5 (fly)

C
6 (land)
7 (open)

D
8 (get out)
9 (talk) Hello!
10 (write)

Ask your neighbour some questions.

A: They're flying into space. Which picture is it?   **B:** Picture two.

You can check your answers with the cassette.

5 It's much bigger!

Comparatives

Extra practice • WB Ex. 9, 10
Extra practice • TB Ws. 2.3

What can you say about these things?

1 PLUTO 1,145 km / MARS 6,794 km (big)

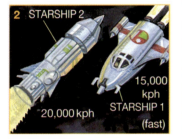
2 STARSHIP 2 15,000 kph / STARSHIP 1 20,000 kph (fast)

3 TELSTAR 3 $32 million / TELSTAR 2 $21 million (expensive)

4 MERCURY 430°C / EARTH 45°C (hot)

6 Can you complete the table?

Comparatives and superlatives

Complete the table with the correct form of the comparatives and superlatives.
Example: Mars is bigger than Pluto. Jupiter is the biggest planet.

Adjective	Comparative	Superlative
big	bigger	the biggest
fast		
hot		
sunny		
easy		
expensive		
interesting		

7 Your Language Record

Now complete your *Language Record* on page 22.

Language Record

The world of people and places

The Present simple Write some more examples.

I You We You They	don't	play tennis every day. work in a restaurant. .... play tennis every day. work in a restaurant.

He She		plays tennis every day. works in a restaurant. ....
	doesn't	play tennis every day. work in a restaurant.

The world of nature

The Present simple: questions Write some more examples.

	do/does	*subject*	*verb*
How many legs	does	an insect	have?
Where	do	leopards	live?
What			
How much			
When			
Why			

Personal pronouns Complete the table.

Example: *Possessive adjective* That's **my** book. *Object pronoun* Please give it to **me**.

I	my	me
you	your	....
he	....	him
she	....	her
it	its	it
we	our	....
you	....	....
they	....	them

The world of science

Complete the tables.

I'm (I'm not) You're (you aren't) He .... She .... It .... We .... You .... They	going to bed. opening the door. getting out of the rocket. talking to someone. ....

Adjective	Comparative	Superlative
fast	faster	the fastest
small	....	....
easy	....	....
interesting	....	....

Theme A
A good life

Unit ☐
Unit ☐
Unit ☐
Unit ☐
Unit ☐

Take a look at Theme A

Where can you find the pictures? Write the Unit number.
Skim through Units 3 and 4. What can you learn about?
Scan Units 3 and 4. Can you find:
   a puzzle?   a song?   a game?
What is on page 29, page 34 and page 35?
What are they for?
What can you do in Unit 5?

Topic 3 Sports for everybody

Sports and health; curriculum links with Sports and Health Education

1 Sports and you

Discussion
Extra practice • WB Ex. 3

Discuss these questions with your class.

Do you do any sports?
How often do you do them?
Which sports do you like doing?
Do you hate doing any sports?
Why do people do sports?
How do different sports make you strong?

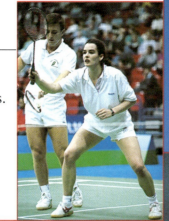

2 Sports that make you strong and flexible

Thinking and discussing

Work with your neighbour.
Look at the list of sports below.

How much energy do you need for each sport?
Put 1 (a little) to 3 (a lot).
Do they make you strong and flexible?
Put one tick √ (a little), two ticks √√, or three ticks √√√ (a lot).

Sport	How much energy do you need?	Does it make you: strong?	flexible?
Badminton	2	√√	√√√
Cycling	2	√√√	√
Fishing	1	√	√
Football			
Golf	2	√√	√√
Running			
Squash			
Swimming			
Table Tennis	1	√	√√
Walking	2	√	√

Compare your ideas with the rest of the class.

Say it clearly!

/ɪŋ/
swimm**ing**
fish**ing**
runn**ing**
cycl**ing**

/ɔː/
sp**o**rts
footb**a**ll
w**a**lking

24 Theme A

3 Sports for health!

Reading
Extra practice •
WB Ex. 1, 2

Read Part 1 of the magazine page about sports and health.
Check your answers to Exercise 2.

4 Anaerobic and aerobic exercise

Read Part 2 of the magazine page. Is football or swimming better for you?
Look at the list of sports in Exercise 2. Are they more anaerobic or aerobic?

SPORTS FOR HEALTH!

1

Swimming is an excellent way to keep fit. It makes your body very flexible (✓✓✓) and can make your body very strong (✓✓✓). Energy level: **2**

Squash is now a very popular game. It is also a very good way to become strong (✓✓) and flexible (✓✓), but you need a lot of energy. Energy level: **3**

Football is popular all over the world. You need a lot of energy to play football well, but anybody can start playing. It makes your legs and your body very strong (✓✓✓). It also helps to make your body flexible (✓✓). Energy level: **2**

Running is a good way to keep fit. Anyone can do it. Running can help to make you strong (✓✓✓). It is very good for your legs, for your heart and your lungs. It also helps to make your body flexible (✓). Energy level: **2**

2

FOOTBALL OR SWIMMING: WHICH IS BETTER FOR YOU?

There are two types of exercise:
anaerobic and **aerobic**.

Football and squash are **anaerobic** exercises. In anaerobic exercises, you move suddenly and quickly. They make your muscles stronger but they don't help your heart very much.

Swimming and running are **aerobic** exercises. In aerobic exercises, you move all the time. They make your heart stronger and they improve your blood circulation.

HOW DO AEROBIC EXERCISES HELP?

Aerobic exercises are better for you. You breathe more oxygen, your heart works hard and this helps your body.

1 You breathe oxygen into your lungs.
2 The oxygen goes into your blood and then to your heart.
3 The heart sends your blood around your body.
4 Your body takes oxygen out of your blood and puts carbon dioxide (CO_2) into it.
5 Your blood goes back to your heart and then to your lungs.
6 You breathe CO_2 out of your lungs.

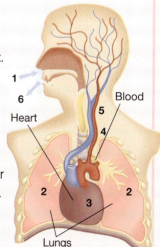

 You can listen to the article on the cassette.

5 Decide …

Choose an exercise. You can work by yourself, with a partner or in a small group.

Exercise 5.1 is about vocabulary.
Exercise 5.2 gives you writing practice about a sport.
Exercise 5.3 gives you writing practice about your favourite sports person or team.

5.1 What's the word?   *Vocabulary*

Can you find nine words in this box from the 'Sports for health' article?
They go across (→), down (↓), and at an angle (↘). Here are some clues:

1 We breathe with our l _ _ _ _

2 h _ _ _ _

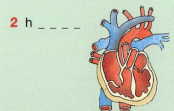

3 Swimming makes your body f _ _ _ _ _ _ _

4 l _ _ _

```
A E F G E G L Y U T F R H
H N E S H L W J K O L K V
Q J W S T R E S R A E G J
J O B H W R R G I U X J H
J Y J A K O O W S T I E E
N B B C G T Y N R D B E A
M L B O D Y I O G S L S L
F S G E T E F H A S E A T
J H S J J S L U N G S A H
E X C E L L E N T N A L T
H E A R T T M U S C L E S
```

5 Sport for h _ _ _ _ _!

6 m _ _ _ _ _ _

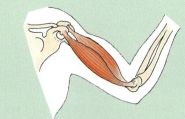

7 Sport can make your b _ _ _ strong and flexible.

8 Running is an e _ _ _ _ _ _ _ _ _ way to keep fit.

9 Football makes your legs s _ _ _ _ _

Now choose some more words and make your own word puzzle.
Draw the clues, or write them in English or your language.
Give your puzzle to other students or put it in your class *Exercise Box*.

5.2 Write about a sport   *Guided writing*

Look back at Part 1 of the article in Exercise 4 and read about each sport again.
Choose another sport from the table in Exercise 2 and write a short paragraph about it.
You can add your own ideas.

How is the sport good for your health?   What do you like about it?
How much energy do you need?   Where can you do it?

5.3 A sports team or person you like   *Free writing*

Think about a sports person or sports team that you like.
Write a short paragraph about them. You can say:

What they play   Who they play for   How good they are   Why you like them
What their best game is   What you want them to do

6 Sing a song! Sports for everybody

Listen to 'Sports for everybody' and sing it with your class. The words to this song are on page 154.

7 The life of a champion swimmer

Discussion; reading
Extra practice •
WB Ex. 4, 7

7.1 Susan Spencer, swimmer

Susan Spencer is 14 years old. She is still at school but she is also a champion swimmer in her country, England. Susan wants to swim in the Olympics.

> What do you think?
> How often does Susan go swimming? When?
> Does she do any other exercise, do you think?
> How is her life different from yours?

Discuss your ideas with the rest of the class.

7.2 Swimming for gold

Read about a day in Susan's life. Can you answer the questions in Exercise 7.1 now?
Why is Susan training so much?

SWIMMING FOR GOLD

A day in the life of Susan Spencer

Susan Spencer, just 14 years old, is one of England's top swimmers. Susan wants to swim for England in the Olympic games and win a gold medal. Susan's life is probably very different from yours. Her day starts at 4.00 am, when she gets up and begins training. She has the same timetable for every day. She swims 400 lengths (20 kilometres) and still has time for school work!

04.00 – 04.30	Susan gets up.
04.30 – 05.00	She goes to the swimming pool.
05.00 – 08.30	Susan swims 200 lengths – that's 10,000 metres or 10 kilometres.
08.30 – 09.00	She has a light breakfast and then goes to school.
09.00 – 15.30	Susan is at school. She does her homework at lunchtime.
15.30 – 18.00	She goes back to the swimming pool and swims another 200 lengths.
18.00 – 18.30	Susan does more exercises.
19.00 – 20.00	She gets back home, has her dinner and then does some more exercises. She lifts weights until 8 o'clock.
20.00 –	Bedtime. Susan sleeps for 8 hours before she starts swimming again!

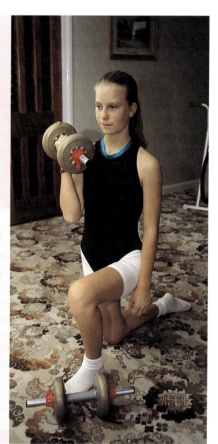

What do you think about Susan's life?
Do you think it is exciting? Do you think she has many friends?

8 Decide ...

Choose an exercise. You can work by yourself, with a partner or in a small group.

Exercise 8.1 practises speaking.
Exercise 8.2 practises speaking and writing.
Exercise 8.3 ... Do it yourself!

8.1 An interview *Speaking*

Imagine that you are interviewing Susan Spencer. Prepare some questions to ask her.
For example:

> What time do you get up, Susan?

> Do you swim at the weekend?

One of you is Susan and the other one is a magazine reporter.
Practise your interview and then act it out for the class.

8.2 Interview your neighbour *Writing*

Talk to your neighbour. Ask each other about your favourite day and what you do.
For example:

> Which is your favourite day?

> What time do you get up?

> What do you do?

Make notes about what your neighbour says.
Then, write the first paragraph of a short magazine article.

A DAY IN THE LIFE OF ...

8.3 Do it yourself! *DIY*

Decide what you want to do and then ask your teacher.
You can use the *Ideas list* on pages 150–1 to make an exercise for your class *Exercise Box*.

9 Your Language Record

Now complete your *Language Record*.

Time to spare? Choose one of these exercises.

1 Write an exercise for your class *Exercise Box* (use the *Ideas list* on pages 150–1) or choose one to do. Check your answers on the back of the paper.
2 Look at Exercise 5.2 again and choose another sport to write about.
3 Look at the Unit again. Write five questions for other students to answer.
  For example:

  What does Susan Spencer do at 8.30 in the morning?
  What is CO_2?

Language Record

Write the meaning of the words in your language.

Word	Meaning	Example
flexible		Swimming makes you very flexible.
health		Sports are good for your health.
homework		Susan does her homework at school.
How many …?		How many sports do you do?
How much …?		How much energy do you need for football?
popular		Football is a very popular sport.
probably		Susan's life is probably very different from your life.
quickly		In football, you run quickly.
suddenly		In anaerobic sports, you often move suddenly.
the heart		Running is good for your heart.
get up		Susan gets up at 4.00 am.
help		Cycling can help to make you stronger.
improve		Swimming improves your blood circulation.
lift		Susan lifts weights.
keep fit		It is important to keep fit.

Choose five more words from the box. Add their meanings and examples.

fishing   walking   lungs   excellent   anybody   blood   breathe   hard   another

Your own notes

Unit 3   Topic   29

4 Language focus

Verb + '-ing'; adverbs; classroom phrases

1 Susan Spencer, the swimmer

Reading and listening
Extra practice • WB Ex. 1

🎧 Peter Black talked to Susan Spencer about her training.
Read (and listen) to what she said. Answer the questions.

What does Susan say about:
– her training?
  She says she started training when she was about nine.

– swimming?
  She says …

– school?

– homework?

– her friends?

Interview with Susan Spencer

PETER: When did you start training?
SUSAN: Well, I started training when I was about nine. At first, only for about an hour every day.
PETER: But now you do five hours every day.
SUSAN: That's right.
PETER: Do you enjoy training?
SUSAN: Oh, yes! I love it. I really love swimming.
PETER: What about school?
SUSAN: Well, I don't mind going to school. I hate doing homework, but school's OK.
PETER: Is it difficult to train so much and do your school work?
SUSAN: It's difficult, yes, but it's not impossible. I stopped going out with my friends so much. Now I have more time to train.
PETER: What do you do in your free time, Susan?
SUSAN: Free time? What's that?!

2 I love swimming

2.1 Some 'special' verbs

'Special' verbs: verbs + '-ing'
Extra practice •
WB Ex. 2,3
Extra practice • TB
Ws. 4.1

In English, there are some 'special' verbs that usually have '-ing' after them.
For example:

  I *love* swimm*ing*.
  I *started* train*ing* when I was nine.

'love' and 'start' are 'special' verbs.
Look back at Exercise 1.
Can you find more 'special' verbs?

30 Theme A

2.2 What do you think?

Talk to your neighbour. Ask each other about what you like.
What do you think about:

- listening to music?
- playing (football, basketball, etc.)?
- doing Maths?
- doing your homework?
- reading?
- learning English?
- going to school?

I love -ing …

I like -ing …

I don't mind -ing …

I hate -ing …

2.3 Write about your opinions

Write a sentence about some of the things in Exercise 2.2.

I like listening to music very much.
I don't mind doing my homework.

Show your work to your neighbour.
Help each other with spelling and grammar.
Ask your teacher for help.

3 'Quickly', 'suddenly' and 'quietly'

Adverbs with '-ly', '-ily'

Extra practice • WB Ex. 4,5
Extra practice • TB Ws. 4.2

3.1 What do you say?

How do you
say these sentences
in your language?

In football, you need to run quickly.

In anaerobic sports, you move suddenly.

In fishing, you need to wait quietly.

Words like 'quickly', 'suddenly' and 'quietly' are called *adverbs*.
They tell you *how* somebody does something.

He walks slowly.

He drives dangerously.

Come quietly now, sir.

Say it clearly!

/li:/
quickly
quietly

Unit 4 Language focus   31

3.2 How to form adverbs

Can you complete the sentences?

He's a very bad driver.
He drives very .... (dangerous)

They are very good singers.
They sing very .... (sweet)

I can understand him easily.
He speaks very .... (slow)

Most adverbs have '**-ly**' on the end. For example:

slow → slow**ly**   quick → quick**ly**   quiet → quiet**ly**   dangerous → dangerous**ly**

Important! Notice where the '**y**' changes to '**i**'! For example:

happy → happ**ily**   easy → eas**ily**   angry → angr**ily**

There are some adverbs that are different.

good → well   fast → fast   hard → hard

Say it clearly!
/ɪli:/
happ**ily**
eas**ily**
angr**ily**

She's a very good driver. She drives very well.

When I run, my heart beats very fast.

He works very hard.

3.3 PRACTICE

What do these notices say? Write down your answers.

quiet   slow   careful   loud   quick

3.4 Play a game!

Choose a phrase and mime it to the class. They have to guess what you are doing.

walk slowly   work happily   open something carefully   shout loudly   drive fast   drive dangerously

read something slowly   work angrily   drive angrily   draw something carefully   talk slowly   talk quietly

walk quickly   open something slowly   read something carefully   work hard   write something slowly

You're talking slowly!   You're driving dangerously!   You're reading something carefully!   You're working hard!

4 Out and about with English

Classroom phrases
Extra practice • WB Ex. 5

4.1 What can you say?

What can you say in your English lesson in these situations?

a You don't understand a word.
b You can't hear.
c You want a dictionary.
d You don't know how to write a word.

4.2 In class

Listen. Alison and Will are in a Mathematics lesson.

What's Alison's problem? What questions does she ask Will?
What questions could she ask the teacher instead of Will?

TEACHER: *Right now. This line is the diameter. We can call it 'd'. Now as you know, you use the formula πd to calculate the circumference of the circle …*

ALISON: What did she say?
WILL: She said that's the diameter.
ALISON: I know that. What does 'pi' mean?
WILL: I don't know. Ask her.
ALISON: No. You ask her.
WILL: No. You ask her.
ALISON: No, Miss.

TEACHER: *Good. Now, for homework, I want you to practise that. Do Exercises 7 and 8 on pages 45 and 46. For next Monday, OK?*

ALISON: What page did she say?
WILL: Page 45.
ALISON: I know that. What was the other page she said?
WILL: I don't know. I didn't hear. What page are we on now?

ALISON: Yes, Miss?
TEACHER: Are you listening?
ALISON: Yes, Miss.
TEACHER: Good. Now tell us what it means.
ALISON: It means … er … what did you say, Miss?
TEACHER: Alison!

TEACHER: *Here's an example. If the diameter is 3 cm then the circumference is…*

… the circumference of this circle is 9.4 cm. That's not too difficult, is it, Alison?

TEACHER: *Good. Now look at page 53. This is a new topic. We're going to look at the area of triangles. First, do you remember what an equilateral triangle is? Anybody? Do you remember what an equilateral triangle is? Alison?*

Unit 4 Language focus   33

4.3 If you don't know, ask!

Here are some more situations. What can you say to the teacher? Choose a phrase.

a You don't know how to say a word in English.
b You have finished your work.
c You want to know if your answer is correct.
d You didn't hear the teacher.
e The teacher is talking too fast.

5 Do it yourself!

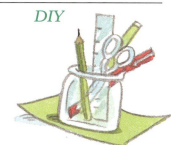

DIY

Look back at Units 1–4. What practice do *you* need? What would *you* like to do?

| write an exercise | sing a song | play a game | write a letter | make a puzzle |
| make a dialogue | discuss something | make a test | read something | ... *you decide!* |

Plan by yourself or with other students what you will do after Unit 7. Make some notes in the space in the *Do it yourself* plan on page 42.

6 Your Language Record

Now complete your *Language Record*.

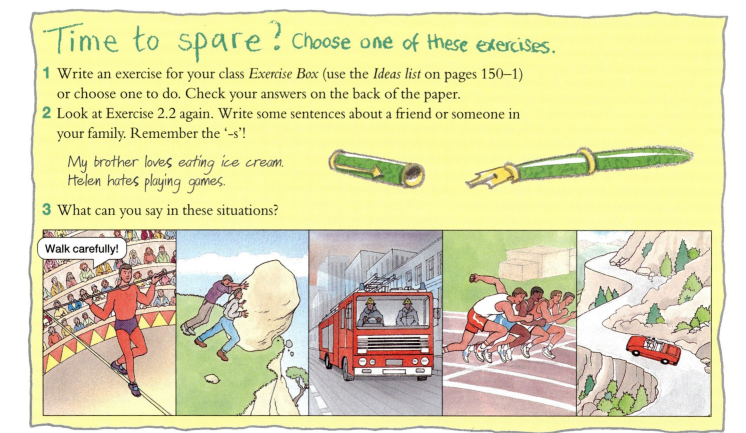

Time to spare? Choose one of these exercises.

1 Write an exercise for your class *Exercise Box* (use the *Ideas list* on pages 150–1) or choose one to do. Check your answers on the back of the paper.
2 Look at Exercise 2.2 again. Write some sentences about a friend or someone in your family. Remember the '-s'!

   My brother loves eating ice cream.
   Helen hates playing games.

3 What can you say in these situations?

Walk carefully!

Language Record

Your own phrase book! CLASSROOM PHRASES

Add more phrases. Write the meaning in your language.

> How do you pronounce this word? ....
> Can you check this? ....
> Sorry, I don't understand. ....
> Can you repeat that? ....
> ....

Write some more examples.
'*Special*' *verbs* + '*-ing*'
  I love swimm*ing*.   I hate .... *ing* ....   I like .... *ing* ....
  I don't mind .... *ing* ....   I started .... *ing* ....

Complete the table.

Adverbs with '-ly'			
She's a careful driver. → She drives very *carefully*.			
slow → *slowly*	quick →	dangerous →	quiet → ....

Adverbs with '-ily'	*Adverbs that are different*.
This is an easy exercise. I can do it very *easily*.	He's a good cook. He cooks very *well*.
happy → .... angry →	fast → .... hard → ....

Revision box Names of animals; 'some' and 'any'

1 Find these animals in the picture.

   kangaroos elephants parrots
   crocodiles bees monkeys
   horses cows lions dolphins

2 Complete the sentence.

   Usually, you use 'some' in **positive** sentences (e.g. There are some kangaroos in the picture). You use 'any' in .... (e.g. Are there any bats?) and in .... (e.g. There aren't any people).

3 Write these words on a piece of paper. Then look at the picture for 15 seconds.

   elephants fish parrots dogs giraffes whales bees sharks cows lions

Close the book and test your memory! Write a sentence about each animal on your list. For example:

There are some elephants in the picture.

Activity 5 A good life

Making a poster
Extra practice • WB Unit 5

You will need: some large pieces of paper, pens, glue, scissors and pictures.

Before your lesson: planning and collecting pictures for your poster

1 What do you need for a good life?

Work with your class. Brainstorm the things that you need for 'a good life'. Make an idea map on the board.

Why is each point important? How many points can you think of?

2 Work in a small group

In your group, choose two or three points each.
Decide what pictures you need for your poster.

3 Collect some pictures

Collect the pictures that you need.
You can use:

photographs …

drawings …

or magazine pictures

Bring your pictures to your Activity lesson.

36   Theme A

In your lesson: writing and showing your posters

4 Write about your pictures

In your group, show your pictures to each other.
Decide what you can say about the pictures.
Decide who can write about each point.
Help each other with spelling, grammar and vocabulary.

Stick your pictures and your writing on your poster paper.

5 Talk about your posters

When you are ready, put your posters on the wall of your class.
Look at the other posters.
Talk about them.
What are the *three* most important things for a good life, do you think?

6 Evaluation

Discuss with the people in your class.

> Did you work well in your group?
> Was it difficult to write? Why?
> How can you do it better next time?

6 Culture matters: At school in the United States

School in the United States and in your country
WB Unit 6:
Help yourself with vocabulary

1 Your school day
Discussion

What time do you begin and finish school each day?
How does your school day begin? Do you eat anything at school? What? When?
How many lessons do you have each day?

2 Lee's school
Reading

With your neighbour, read about Lee Bier's school day.
How many things are different from your school? Make a list.
Compare your ideas with the rest of your class.

Lee goes to a 'Junior High School' near Portland, Maine in the North East of the United States. The school has 1100 students between 12 and 15 years old. Lee goes to school from Monday to Friday, from 8.00am until 2.00pm.

Lee's day begins in his 'home class'. This is the room that his group uses most of the time. Here, his teacher checks that everybody is there. Then they listen to announcements from the loudspeaker and they all say the 'Pledge of Allegiance' to the United States flag.

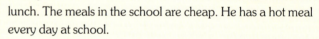

After that, he has three lessons. At about 11.00am he has a long break for lunch until about 12.00. There is a canteen where he buys his lunch. The meals in the school are cheap. He has a hot meal every day at school.

After his meal, there are lots of activities in the school that he can do. Lee likes playing in the school band at lunchtime. His lessons begin again at about 12.00.

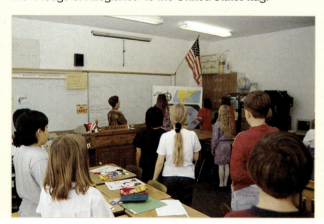

You can hear the text on the cassette.

38 Theme A

3 Lee's school subjects

Reading

Lee has five lessons every day except Wednesday. On Wednesday, Lee does sports in the afternoon. He likes playing American football, basketball and baseball. Lee's favourite subjects are Science and Mathematics. On Thursday he has 'Shop'. In Shop, he enjoys making things with wood and metal. Lee has short tests or 'quizzes' every week in each subject. He doesn't usually have any homework. Instead, he is always learning things for the quizzes. He hates them!

Here is Lee's timetable. Which do you think is his favourite day?

Time	Monday	Tuesday	Wednesday	Thursday	Friday
8.00	Home class	Home class	Home class	Home class	Home class
8.15	Algebra	Geography	Algebra	Algebra	P.E.
9.10	Drama	Drama	Drama	Science	Spanish
10.05	US History	US History	US History	Science	Library
11.00	LUNCH	LUNCH	LUNCH	LUNCH	LUNCH
12.05	Spanish	Art	Sport	Shop	Geography
12.55	Geography	Music	Sport	Shop	Art

Do you have homework or quizzes? How many differences can you find with your school timetable?

4 School rules

Reading and discussing

Lee's school gives each student some rules when they start. Read Lee's school rules. Do you think they are good rules? Do you have the same rules in your school?

You can hear the rules on the cassette.

HILLSIDE JUNIOR HIGH SCHOOL

RULES

1. All students must look clean and tidy.
2. Students must not bring any knives or any other weapons to school.
3. Students must not eat or drink in the school buildings, except in the school canteen. Students must not smoke.
4. Students must not run or shout in the school buildings.
5. All students must bring the books, pens, paper and equipment they need for the day.
6. All students must put their things in their locker in the hall.

5 Across cultures

Writing

How big is your school?
What subjects do you have on your timetable?
What rules do you have in your school? (Are they good rules, do you think?)
Work with your neighbour.
Write your timetable, your school rules or a short description of your school in English.

7 Revision and evaluation

Revision of Units 3–6
Extra practice • WB Unit 7
Test yourself

1 How well do you know it?

Self-assessment

How well do you think you know the English you learnt in Units 3–6? Put a tick (✓) in the table.

	very well	OK	a little
Talk about your day			
Talk about your likes and dislikes			
Describe how somebody does something (quickly, slowly, etc.)			
New words			

Now choose some sections to revise and practise.

2 A life of luxury

Describe your day;
Present simple revision
Extra practice • WB Ex. 2, 3

Work with your neighbour.
One of you do Exercise A and the other one do Exercise B.

A Imagine that you are a very, very rich person!
You don't work.
Every day, you do exactly what *you* want to do.
What do you do?
What is a typical day for you?
What are your plans for the future?
Write down some ideas.

B You work for a TV station.
You are going to interview the richest person in your country.
You want to know:
– what he/she does every day.
– what he/she does with his/her money.
What questions can you ask?
Write down your ideas.

When you are ready, talk to each other!

My day
I get up at 10 or 11 o'clock
I have breakfast in my garden.
Then, I ....

Every day
What time do you get up?
Do you do any sports?
What do you eat? Where do you eat?

Theme A

3 What do you think?

Likes and dislikes; verb + '-ing'
Extra practice • WB Ex. 4

Look at these pictures. What do you think about them? Write about each one. For example:

I love eating ice cream. I think it's delicious.

1 Ice cream
2 Homework
3 Cleaning
4 Dentist
5 Reading
6 Dancing

Find out what other people in your class think.

4 What's the missing word?

Adverbs: '-ly', '-ily' and exceptions

Simon and Sue are talking about some music. Can you fill in the missing word?

SIMON: Did you like that, Sue?
SUE: Yes, but I thought they played it too ......(1)...... (fast).
SIMON: No, they didn't. They played it too ......(2)...... (slow). I thought it was terrible!
SUE: Terrible?! They played ......(3)...... (beautiful).
SIMON: I thought the singer sang very ......(4)...... (bad). He's got a terrible voice.
SUE: Well, I liked it. They play very ......(5)...... (good).
SIMON: No, they don't!
SUE: Yes, they do!

5 What's the word?

Can you complete the puzzle?

1 Aerobic exercises make your h.............. stronger.
2 You don't need much e.............. for fishing.
3 Swimming i.............. your blood circulation.
4 A red liquid.
5 Any.............. can start playing football.
6 Susan .... weights after dinner.
7 Swimming makes your body f.............. .
8 The school day in the USA and England is very d.............. .
9 In anaerobic exercises you move ....

Look back at the chart in Exercise 1. Were you right?

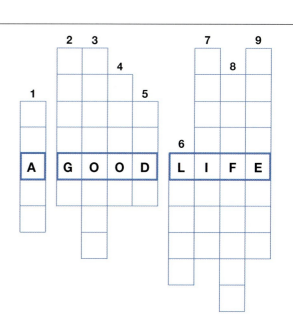

Unit 7 Revision and evaluation 41

6 Looking back at Units 3–6

Evaluation

6.1 Group discussion

Form groups of three or four students.
Decide, with your class, which groups will look at:

Unit 3 *or* Unit 4 *or* Units 5 and 6.

In your group, decide who will report back to the class.
Look through the Units you chose and talk about these questions:

Unit 3	Unit 4	Units 5 and 6
Did you think the topics were interesting? Did you have enough time to do the exercises?	Were the grammar exercises clear? Do you need to practise some more again?	Did you enjoy the activity? Did you learn anything new about school life in the United States?

6.2 Your own ideas

Write down any suggestions you have for future lessons.
Give your paper to your teacher at the end of the lesson.

7 Learning vocabulary

Work by yourself.
Answer the questions with a tick (√).

	always	often	sometimes	never
1 Do you forget new words?	☐	☐	☐	☐
2 Do you have problems with spelling?	☐	☐	☐	☐
3 Do you have problems with pronunciation?	☐	☐	☐	☐
4 Do you make mistakes with vocabulary?	☐	☐	☐	☐
5 Do you practise vocabulary at home?	☐	☐	☐	☐

Compare your answers with your neighbour and other people in your class. Look at the Workbook Unit 6 for ideas about learning vocabulary.

Open plan

Do it yourself!

See Unit 4 Exercise 5.

Make notes about what you plan to do.

Do it yourself!
PLAN
Bring to class:
Do in class:

Theme B
Life on Earth

Unit ☐

Unit ☐

Unit ☐

Unit ☐

Unit ☐

Take a look at Theme B
Where can you find the pictures? Write the Unit number.
Scan Units 8 and 9 for this information:
 Where are the rainforests? Name four types of dinosaur.
 Name a plant that grows in Java.
What can you do in Unit 10?

Topic 8 In a rainforest

Rainforests and trees; curriculum links with Environmental Science, Natural History and Prehistory

1 What do you know about rainforests?

Discussion

Look at these pictures.

- What is a rainforest?
- What types of animals live there?
- What plants live there?
- Why are the rainforests important?

Tell the class your ideas.

2 In the rainforest

🎧 Listen to some sounds from a rainforest.
What can you hear?
What do you think each thing is doing?

I can hear ...

Compare answers with the rest of the class.

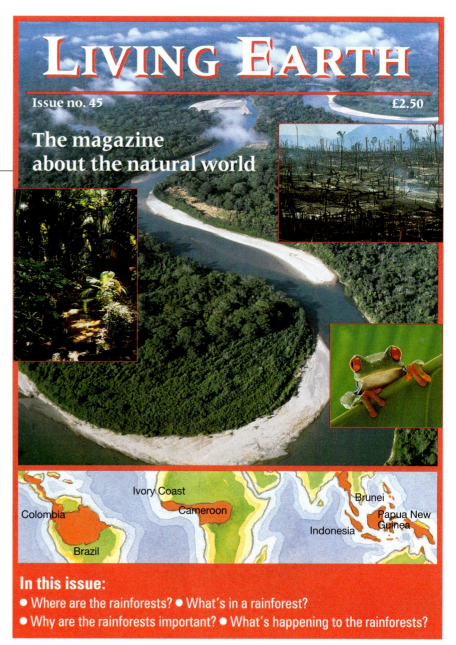

3 Why are the rainforests important?

Reading
Extra practice •
WB Exs. 1–4

3.1 The magazine questions

Look at the questions on the magazine cover in Exercise 1.
What do you think the magazine tells you?

44   Theme B

3.2 Read about the rainforests

Here is a part of the article about rainforests. First, read it all the way through. Talk to your neighbour about what you understand.

Now, with your neighbour, make a list of the things that you don't understand.

> Things we don't understand
> Rainforests cover six per cent of the Earth's surface.
> breathe

Look at the text again. Can you guess the meaning of the words?

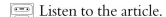 Listen to the article.

4 Decide …

THE RAINFORESTS: WHY ARE THEY IMPORTANT?

1 Where are the rainforests?
Rainforests cover six per cent of the Earth's surface. There are rainforests in many parts of the world but the biggest forests are in South America, Africa and South East Asia. There aren't any rainforests in Europe or North America.

2 What's in the rainforests?
About 75% of all the types of animals that we know come from rainforests. Thousands and thousands of animals live in rainforests. There are many very beautiful birds, insects and reptiles. Many of them live in the trees, over 30 metres from the ground. There are also thousands of different plants — and lots of tall trees! It is always hot in a rainforest and the ground is always wet. It is also dark.

3 Why are the rainforests important?
The rainforests are very important for us. We need them! The trees and other plants in the forest help to make the air that we breathe. They also help to control the weather. They give us wood, rubber, fruits and many of our medicines.

4 What's happening to the rainforests?
Unfortunately, in many places, the rainforests are in danger. For example, many years ago there was a large rainforest in Java. There were thousands of different plants and animals in the forest, but now there is nothing. People chopped down the trees because they wanted to grow rice. They also planted rubber trees to make rubber. Many animals lived in the rainforest. Some of them went to other parts of Java but many of them disappeared — forever. The same thing is happening now in many other parts of the world. The rainforests are in danger!

Rubber and many of our medicines come from the rainforests.

Choose an exercise. You can work by yourself, with a partner or in a small group.

Exercise 4.1 is about vocabulary.
Exercise 4.2 checks your comprehension.
Exercise 4.3 gives you writing practice.

4.1 Words in groups   *Vocabulary*

Look at these words. Can you put them into three groups?
(Note! Some words can go into two groups.)

animals   wood
birds   dark
trees   air   hot
rain   rubber
plants   fruits
tall   medicines
wet   insects

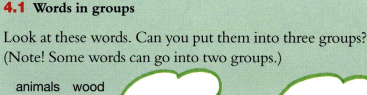

Say it clearly!

/e/ ins**e**ct, m**e**dicine, w**e**t;
/ɑː/ d**a**rk, pl**a**nt;
/æ/ **a**nimal

Unit 8   Topic   45

4.2 True or false?

Reading comprehension

Look back at the article in Exercise 3.2.
Are these sentences true or false? If they are false, put them right.

- a The ground is always hot in the rainforest.
- b There are rainforests in Asia.
- c Seventy-five per cent of all animals live in rainforests.
- d Many medicines come from rainforests.
- e There is a very big rainforest in Java.

Write four or five more 'true or false' sentences.
Give them to some other students to read, or put them in your class *Exercise Box*.

4.3 In the rainforest

Guided writing

Imagine that you are walking in a rainforest. It's hot and dark. You can hear lots of noises. The ground is very wet. You know that there are a lot of wild animals near you. What can you see? What can you hear? How do you feel?
Write about your ideas.

I'm walking in the forest. I can see ... I can hear ... I feel ... I want to ....

5 How do the rainforests make rain?

Reading

Can you put the pieces in the correct places?

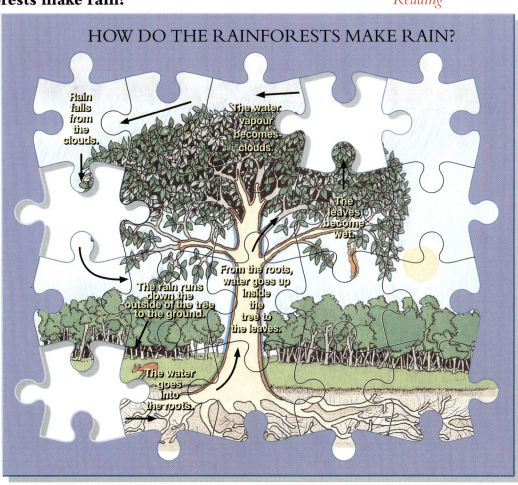

You can check your answers with the cassette.

6 Sing a song! Mother forest

🎧 Listen to 'Mother forest' and sing it with your class. The words are on page 154.

7 The oldest living things on Earth …

Listening
Extra practice • WB Ex. 5

7.1 What do you think?

What do *you* think are the oldest living things on Earth?
On the cassette, you can hear Anne Briggs.
She says the following words. What do you think she tells us?

| 4,000 years old | before people lived in towns | very slowly | 14 metres |
| a rainforest in Australia | 150 million years old | dinosaurs lived |

7.2 The Living Planet

🎧 'The Living Planet' is a radio programme.
Jack Fenton is talking to Anne Briggs about the oldest living things on Earth. Listen.
Are your answers to Exercise 7.1 correct?

The Bristlecone Pines, California

7.3 Listen again

Listen to the programme again once or twice.
What does Anne Briggs say about the following?

1994   the continents   dinosaurs   the climate   plants and animals

Say it clearly!

/wəz/ **was**; /wə/ **were**;
/ɪd/ start**ed**;
/d/ discover**ed**, live**d**,
change**d**, die**d**

8 Decide …

Choose an exercise. You can work by yourself, with a partner or in a small group.

Exercise 8.1 practises writing.
Exercise 8.2 practises vocabulary.
Exercise 8.3 … Do it yourself!

8.1 A fantastic discovery

Imagine that you work for a newspaper in Australia.
Write a news story about the Wollemi Pines.

How did they discover them?
Where did they discover them?
What do they look like?
How tall are they?
What colour are they?
Draw a picture of the trees and write a short news story.

15 December 19

FANTASTIC DISCOVERY IN WOLLEMI!

The Oldest Trees on Earth

Yesterday, people discovered the oldest trees on Earth.
They discovered them … They are …
The trees started growing in Australia when …

Unit 8   Topic   47

8.2 What's the word? *Vocabulary*

Read the clues and put the words in the puzzle. What word is number 11?

1. The biggest rainforests are in South ....
2. When the .... changed millions of years ago, many plants and animals died.
3. We get a lot of m............ from rainforests.
4. Many rainforests are in d............ .
5. Rain .... from clouds.
6. Clouds are made from water ....
7. The oldest living things on Earth.
8. It grows in Java where the rainforest was.
9. The sun ....
10. The ground in a rainforest is always ....

Now find another long word. For example:

discovery   medicines   dinosaurs   disappeared   Australia

Make a puzzle for other students to do.

8.3 Do it yourself! *DIY*

Decide what you want to do and then ask your teacher.
You can use the *Ideas list* on pages 150–1 to make an exercise for your class *Exercise Box*.

9 Your Language Record

Now complete your *Language Record*.

Time to spare? Choose one of these exercises.

1. Write an exercise for your class *Exercise Box* (use the *Ideas list* on pages 150–1) or choose one to do. Check your answers on the back of the paper.
2. Copy the nine sentences in Exercise 5 on to nine separate pieces of paper. Mix them up and see if you can put them in the correct order.
3. Read the text in Exercise 3.2 again. Write five questions for other students to answer.

Language Record

Write the meaning of the words in your language. Write the missing examples.

Word	Meaning	Example
rainforest		The rainforests give us many important things.
world		There are many countries in the world.
surface		Rainforests cover six per cent of the world's surface.
thousand		There are thousands of different plants in a rainforest.
ground		The ground is always wet.
weather		Rainforests help to control the weather.
root		Trees have roots.
cloud		Rain comes from clouds.
leaf (leaves)		Giraffes eat leaves.
medicine		
inside		
outside		
forever		Some animals in Java disappeared forever.
climate		Millions of years ago, the climate changed a lot.
important		
hot		
dark		
wet		
cover		Rainforests cover a small part of the Earth.
grow		
catch		Trees catch the rain on their leaves.
disappear		Dinosaurs disappeared a long time ago.

Choose five more words from the box. Add their meanings and examples.

| million   plant (noun)   plant (verb)   help   give   chop   something   down   insect   reptile |
| bird   rubber   die |

Your own notes

Unit 8 Topic 49

9 Language focus

Past simple: 'be', regular verbs; inviting and suggesting

1 When the Wollemi Pines started growing

Extra practice • WB Ex. 1

The Wollemi Pines in the Australian rainforest started growing at the time of the dinosaurs. But what do you know about the dinosaurs? Are these sentences true [T] or false [F]?

1. Dinosaurs were reptiles.
2. Some dinosaurs were very small.
3. At the time of the dinosaurs, there was only one continent.
4. Dinosaurs were on Earth for more than 100 million years.
5. Dinosaurs died a long time before people appeared on Earth.
6. Birds lived at the same time as dinosaurs.
7. Dinosaurs lived in all parts of the world.
8. Some dinosaurs moved very quickly.
9. Most dinosaurs did not eat meat.
10. Some scientists think dinosaurs disappeared because a meteor crashed into the Earth.
11. They discovered the first dinosaur bones in England.

Compare your answers with your neighbour and the rest of the class. Your teacher has got the correct answers!

2 More dinosaur facts

Read these descriptions of four dinosaurs. Can you match them to the correct picture?

a. This dinosaur was very small. It was about 50 cm long. It walked on two legs and it had a long, thin tail. It was a meat-eater. It had a lot of teeth. It moved very fast.
b. This dinosaur was very big. It was about 25 metres long. It had a long, heavy body and thick, heavy legs. It had a small head. It walked on four legs and lived near water. It moved very slowly.
c. This dinosaur walked on two legs and on four legs. It was about 2.5 metres tall and about 6 metres long. It had short legs at the front and long legs at the back. It also had triangular 'plates' along its back.
d. This dinosaur was a plant-eater. It was about 2 metres long and it was heavy. It walked on four legs. Its head was very big, almost as long as its body. At the back of its head, it had bones. They looked like a fan.

Compsognathus   Protoceratops   Stegosaurus   Apatosaurus

3 In the dinosaur forest

3.1 'Was' or 'were'?

When do you say 'was'?
When do you say 'were'?
Look at the sentences and complete the ones below.

> Dinosaurs were reptiles.
> We were not alive 150 million years ago.
> I was interested in dinosaurs.
> Some dinosaurs were very small.
> The Compsognathus was very small. It was about 50 cm long.

I	....	
You	were	
He She It	....	very big. very tall. 50 years old.
We	....	
You	were	
They	....	

There .... only one continent 150 million years ago.
There .... many types of dinosaurs.

'was' and 'were'
Extra practice • WB Ex. 2
Extra practice •
TB Ws. 9.1

Say it clearly!

/wəz/ was
/wə/ were

3.2 Spot the difference!

Look at these pictures.
Can you find eight differences
between 'in the morning' and 'in the afternoon'?

In the morning

In the afternoon

Write some sentences about each picture.

In the morning
There was ...
There were ...

Unit 9 Language focus

4 Some more Past tense verbs

Past simple: regular verbs
Extra practice • WB Exs. 3–5
Extra practice • TB Ws. 9.2

4.1 What do you say?

Think about the Past tense in your language.
Do many verbs have the same ending? Which verbs are they?

4.2 The rainforest in Java

In Unit 8 Exercise 3.2 you read about the rainforest in Java.
Read about it again but, this time, find the verbs.

Make a list of the verbs in two columns.
What do you notice about most of the verbs?

INFINITIVE	PAST TENSE
be	was, were
go	went
chop	....
....	....
....	....

4.3 Regular verbs

Many verbs in English are 'regular'. This means that they end with '-ed' in the past.
Look back at the sentences in Exercise 1. Can you find any more regular verbs?

4.4 Say it clearly!

Be careful with the pronunciation of '-ed'!
There are three ways to say it: /ɪd/ as in 'started', /t/ as in 'walked' and /d/ as in 'lived'.

Listen. Match the verbs to the correct pronunciation.

washed   wanted   stayed   played   looked   visited   liked   decided

/ɪd/   /t/   /d/

4.5 How they discovered the Wollemi Pines

Read about how they discovered the Wollemi Pines in the Australian rainforest. Complete the text with the Past tense of the verbs.

David Noble .... (work) for the Australian National Parks Service. One weekend in August 1994, he .... (visit) the Wollemi Park rainforest. He .... (walk) for hours and hours through thick forest. He .... (want) to see what was at the bottom of a valley. With a rope, he .... (climb) 600 metres down the rocks. There, he .... (discover) 42 trees. They .... (look) very strange. Mr Noble .... (collect) some pieces of the trees and then he went back to Sydney. In Sydney, he .... (look) carefully at the trees. He .... (compare) them with tree fossils from prehistoric times. The Wollemi trees and the fossils were exactly the same! They .... (start) growing when dinosaurs .... (live) in Australia. In December 1994, the Australian Government officially said that the Wollemi Pines were a new type of tree – over 150 million years old!

You can check your answers with the cassette.

4.6 SOME MORE PRACTICE

When did you last do the things in the pictures? Write a sentence for each one.

I played football last Saturday.

watch television

paint a picture

walk home

travel by bus

5 Out and about with English

Inviting and suggesting
Extra practice • WB Ex. 6

5.1 What can you say?

If you want to invite someone to your house, what can you say?
Make a list of the phrases you can use.

5.2 Will meets Alison and Nick

Listen. Will is in the street and he meets his friend, Alison. Does Will use the phrases on your list from Exercise 5.1? Who is Nick? Is he a nice person, do you think? What plans do they make?

WILL: Hi, Alison! What are you doing?
ALISON: Hi, Will. We're going home. This is Nick, my cousin.
WILL: Hello, Nick.
NICK: Hello.

WILL: I'm going into town. Why don't you come with me? I want to get tickets for The Mash Boys concert.
NICK: The Mash Boys!
WILL: Yes, they're playing on Saturday. I'm going with Helen.
NICK: Yuck!
ALISON: You said you didn't like The Mash Boys.
WILL: Well, I don't mind them. Helen wants to go. Would you like to come?
ALISON: No thanks, Will.
NICK: The Mash Boys. They're terrible! I hate them. Just a lot of noise!
ALISON: All right, Nick. You're not going to the concert. What are you doing later, Will?
WILL: Nothing. Why don't we meet at my house?
ALISON: Good idea. Shall I tell Helen?
WILL: Fine. Let's meet at around five.
NICK: Tell Helen not to bring any Mash Boys records with her.
ALISON: Oh, be quiet Nick! See you later Will. Bye!
WILL: Bye!

5.3 PRACTICE

Work with a partner. Imagine that you meet each other in the street.
Make a conversation to invite your partner somewhere.
You can change Alison and Will's dialogue.

- Hello. What are you doing?
- I'm …
- Why don't you …?
- Why don't we …?
- Would you like to?
- Let's …

When you are ready, act out your conversation for the class.

6 Do it yourself!

DIY

Look back at Units 8 and 9. What practice do *you* need? What would *you* like to do?

| write an exercise | sing a song | play a game | write a letter | make a puzzle |
| make a dialogue | discuss something | make a test | read something | … *you decide!* |

Plan by yourself or with other students what you will do after Unit 12.
Make some notes in the space in the *Do it yourself* plan on page 62.

7 Your Language Record

Now complete your *Language Record*.

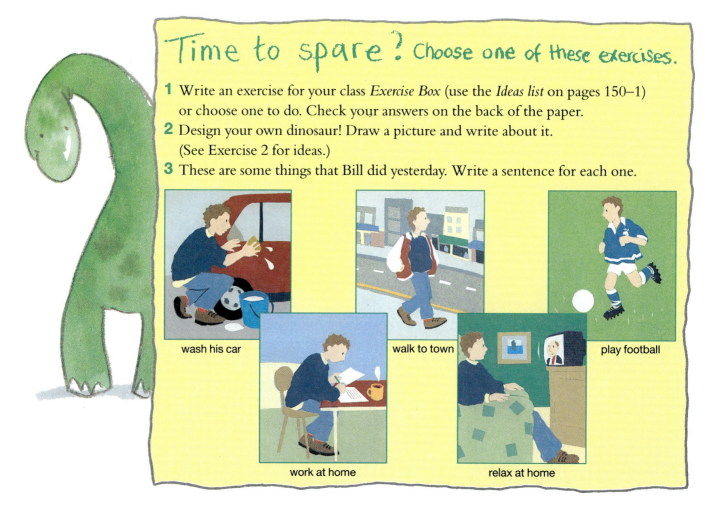

Time to spare? Choose one of these exercises.

1. Write an exercise for your class *Exercise Box* (use the *Ideas list* on pages 150–1) or choose one to do. Check your answers on the back of the paper.
2. Design your own dinosaur! Draw a picture and write about it. (See Exercise 2 for ideas.)
3. These are some things that Bill did yesterday. Write a sentence for each one.

wash his car   walk to town   play football   work at home   relax at home

Language Record

Your own phrase book! SUGGESTING AND INVITING

Add more phrases. Write the meaning in your language.

> Why don't you come with me? ....
> Why don't we meet at my house? ....
> Would you like to come? ....
> Shall I tell …? ....
> Let's meet at around five. ....
> See you later. ....

Complete the table.

I was
You ....
He ⎫
She ⎬ .... 15 years old yesterday
It ⎭
We ....
You ....
They ....
There .... many dinosaurs in England millions of years ago.
There .... a change in the climate.

Complete the examples.
walk: Yesterday, I walked to school.
watch: I .... TV.
play: I .... a game.
visit: I .... my friends.
paint: I .... a picture.
help: I .... my sister with her homework.
cook: My friend .... a meal.

Write /t/, /d/ or /ɪd/ next to each verb to show the pronunciation.

Say it clearly!
/wəz/ was
/wə/ were

Revision box The Present continuous

1 You use the Present continuous to talk about things that are happening now.

   You're reading this!
   You're sitting in an English class.

   How can you describe the Present continuous?

   Subject + +
   You   're   read*ing* this.

2 Play a game. Mime an action. The others in your class have to guess what you are doing.

   You're driving a car!
   You're opening a box!
   You're chopping down a tree!

3 What's happening here?
   Write six sentences about the picture.

Activity 10 Poems from the rainforest

Writing poems
Extra practice •
WB Unit 10

1 The things you remember

🔊 Think about the rainforest and write down the words you can remember. You can listen to the cassette while you think. It has some more sounds from the rainforest and some music from South America on it.

The rainforest — Hot, Dark, Lots of trees, Thousands of animals, Water vapour, Clouds, Rubber

2 Your words

Show your words to your neighbour and look back at Units 8 and 9.
Do you want to add any words?
Talk to your neighbour about what the words mean.

3 In the rainforest

Imagine that you are in a rainforest. It can be now, or in the time of the dinosaurs. What can you hear? What can you see? Is it a nice place or a horrible place? Why?

Imagine that a rainforest can speak.
What does it say? Tell the rest of the class your ideas.

Theme B

4 A poem

Write a poem about your ideas.
You are in a rainforest, or the rainforest speaks.
Read your poem and make changes as you write.

For more ideas, show your poem to your neighbour.
Look back at Units 8 and 9.
Write your poem in a shape.
Choose something from your words in Exercise 1.

🖭 You can listen to the poems on the cassette.

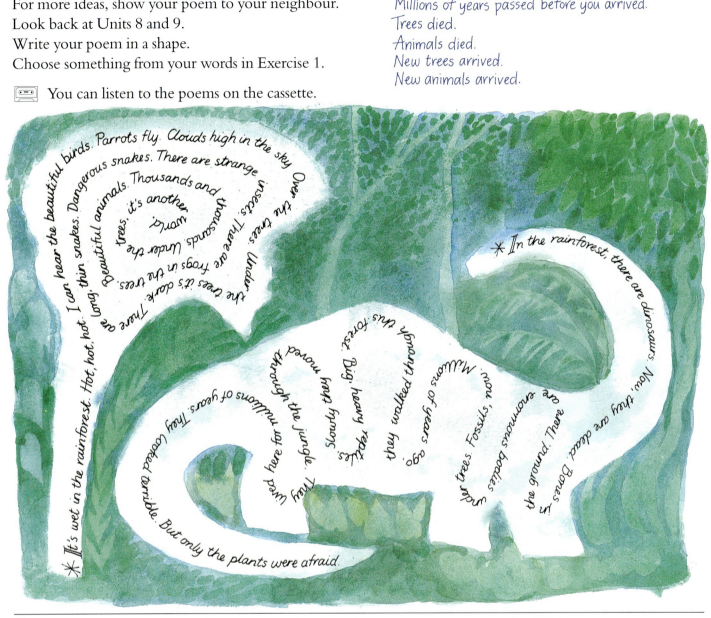

The rainforest speaks
I give you plants for your medesines [medicines]
and I give you rubber for your houses [cars].
There are insects in my trees [birds]
Millions of years passed before you arrived.
Trees died.
Animals died.
New trees arrived.
New animals arrived.

5 Show your poems

Either put your poems on the wall and walk around the class to read the other poems,
or sit in a small group and read your poem to the other students.
Which parts do you like from the other students' poems?

6 Evaluation

Was it easy or difficult to write the poems?

Did you like writing poems?   Would you like to do it again?
How?   Alone?   In a group?   In your book?   On a poster?

11 Culture matters — Discover America!

Physical Geography and Natural History in the United States of America

WB Unit 11: Help yourself with writing

1 Landscape in your country

Do you have many forests, mountains, lakes, rivers or deserts in your country? Where are they?

2 Landscape in the United States

Read about the landscape of the United States. Put symbols on the map to show mountains, volcanoes, lakes, rivers and deserts.

WELCOME to the UNITED STATES!

In the USA you can find some of the most beautiful and spectacular landscape in the world. There's a lot for you to see and do!

In the East
Around the Gulf of Mexico and up to Long Island, the area is very flat, with many, many beaches. If you go west from the coast, you can see the Appalachian Mountains. The Appalachians go from Alabama and Georgia all the way up into Canada. Also in the East you can see the longest river in the United States, the Mississippi River. The Mississippi goes from Minnesota to New Orleans. It is almost 3,800km long. The five biggest lakes in the United States are in the East, near Chicago, Detroit and Duluth.

In the West
West from the Appalachians, the land is very flat and dry and there is a lot of desert. The famous Rocky Mountains begin near Denver in Colorado and go right the way up into Canada. Also in Colorado, south from the Rocky Mountains, there are many beautiful canyons, including the Grand Canyon of the Colorado River. Over in California, you can find fantastic sandy beaches.

Alaska and Hawaii
Alaska and Hawaii are also very beautiful. Alaska has many, many mountains all around the Gulf of Alaska. The highest mountain in the United States, Mount McKinley, is in Alaska. It is over 6,000m high. Hawaii is very different. There you can see many volcanoes, including two active volcanoes, Kilauea and Mauna Loa.

3 Three places to visit

Here are three famous places in the United States. Where are they on the map in Exercise 2?

Where can you:

a see some beautiful colours?
b find information about prehistoric life?
c see hot water that comes from the ground?

Which places would you like to visit?

🎧 You can listen to the texts on the cassette.

DINOSAUR NATIONAL MONUMENT

Millions of years ago, dinosaurs walked all over the United States. Today, at Dinosaur National Monument, on the border between Colorado and Utah, you can see the enormous skeletons of these animals. You can see the complete bones and eggs of many dinosaurs and discover how they lived. Visit the monument and learn about prehistoric life!

The Grand Canyon

Millions of years ago, in the time of the dinosaurs, the Colorado River was much bigger. Today, in the spectacular Grand Canyon, you can see how big it really was. The Canyon is over 349km long and more than 1.5km deep, and 20km wide in places. It has many beautiful colours that change during the day. Come and see one of the wonders of the world in Arizona!

Yellowstone National Park

Come to Wyoming and see the wonders of nature in Yellowstone! In Yellowstone National Park you can see over 200 geysers, including the famous 'Old faithful' geyser. See the ground come alive as hot gases bubble up! Also in the park, there are hundreds of different types of animals, including buffaloes and elks. But be careful — there are many dangerous animals in Yellowstone — watch out for bears!

4 Where are they?

🎧 Listen. A tourist guide is talking about the places in Exercise 3. Where are they?

5 Across cultures

What natural places can you visit near where you live?
Imagine you are a guide. What can you tell tourists?
Say what they can see there and what they can do.
Act out your talk for the class.

You can also collect some pictures and write about them for tourists to read.

Revision and evaluation

Revision of Units 8–11
Extra practice •
WB Unit 12

1 How well do you know it?

Self-assessment

How well do you think you know the English you learnt in Units 8–11? Put a tick (√) in the table.

	very well	OK	a little
'was/were'			
Past simple with regular verbs ('-ed')			
Inviting and suggesting			
New words			

Now choose some sections to revise and practise.

2 Test yourself!

A test

Work with your neighbour and do this short test.

TEST YOURSELF!

A Where were they?

'was/were'

Write four sentences about Pictures A and B.

The .... was/were .... but now ....

B What did they do yesterday?

Regular verbs: '-ed'

Write a sentence about each picture.

Peter ...

Helen ...

Peter ...

Helen ...

60 Theme B

C Let's play football.

Inviting and suggesting

Complete the dialogue. Choose **a**, **b**, **c** or **d**.

a Where can we play?
b Great. Let's meet there in five minutes.
c Nothing.
d OK. Have you got a ball?

JACK: Hello, Lily. What are you doing?
LILY: ....
JACK: Why don't we play football?
LILY: ....
JACK: Yes, at home. I can get it.
LILY: ....
JACK: Let's go to the park.
LILY: ....

D What's the word?

New words

Can you find the words in the puzzle?

a D.................. lived millions of years ago.
b There are a lot of t.................. in a rainforest.
c Rain comes from c.................. .
d At night, it is d.................. .
e B.................. can fly.
f Snakes are r.................. .

```
Y D A B G C L O U D S F
U D I N O S A U R S K T
D E B Y H W I Y E H L H
A J I K I T R E E S K K
R W R J K W J K W J H M
K W D Y T E H U W O K G
E W S Y R E P T I L E S
```

Check your answers on page 142.
Look back at Exercise 1. Were you right?

---

3 Write your own test!

Write a test

Work in small groups.
Look back at Units 8–11 and write part of a test for your class.
Look at the test in Exercise 2 for ideas.
Tell your teacher which part you are doing.

A 'was/were'.
Draw two pictures, one 'Now' and one 'Five minutes ago'.
You can draw a picture of a classroom, a town, some animals in the jungle …

B Past simple with regular verbs ('-ed').
Draw some pictures about a regular verb.

C Inviting and suggesting.
Write a conversation. Take some sentences out.

D New words.
Make a word puzzle. Write some clues.

Check your work and write the answers to your part of the test.
Give the test to your teacher to check and to put together for your class.

4 Looking back at Units 8–11

4.1 Group discussion

Form groups of three or four students.
Decide, with your class, which groups will look at:

Unit 8 *or* Unit 9 *or* Units 10 and 11.

In your group, decide who will report back to the class.
Look through the Units you chose and talk about these questions:

Unit 8	Unit 9	Units 10 and 11
Did you think the topics were interesting? Did you have enough time to do the exercises?	Were the grammar exercises clear? Do you need to practise some more again?	Did you enjoy the activity? Did you learn anything about the United States?

4.2 Your own ideas

Write down any suggestions you have for future lessons.
Give your paper to your teacher at the end of the lesson.

5 Learning to write in English

Work by yourself.
Answer the questions with a tick (√).

	always	often	sometimes	never
1 Do you like writing in English?	☐	☐	☐	☐
2 Is it difficult to write in English?	☐	☐	☐	☐
3 Do you make the same mistakes again and again?	☐	☐	☐	☐
4 When you write something, do you check it?	☐	☐	☐	☐
5 Do you make lists of your mistakes?	☐	☐	☐	☐

Compare your answers with your neighbour and other people in your class. Look at the Workbook Unit 11 for ideas about learning to write in English.

Open plan

Do it yourself!

See Unit 9 Exercise 6.

Make notes about what you plan to do.

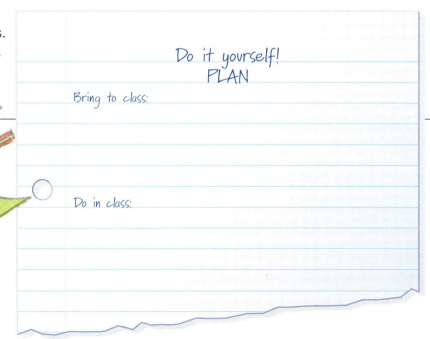

Do it yourself!
PLAN

Bring to class:

Do in class:

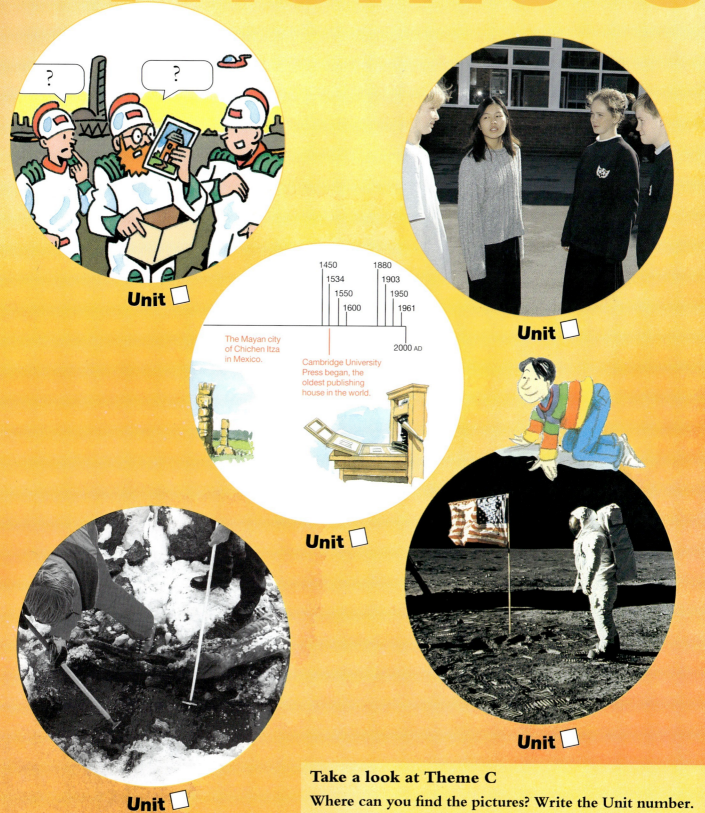

Theme C
Back in time

Unit ☐

Unit ☐

1450
1534
1550
1600
1880
1903
1950
1961
2000 AD

The Mayan city of Chichen Itza in Mexico.

Cambridge University Press began, the oldest publishing house in the world.

Unit ☐

Unit ☐

Unit ☐

Take a look at Theme C
Where can you find the pictures? Write the Unit number. *Skim* through Units 13 and 14. What can you learn about? What can you do in Unit 15?

Topic 13 Detectives of history

Historical discoveries and historical clues; curriculum link with History

1 The history of the world

Discussion
Extra practice • WB Ex. 1

What do you think are the most important inventions in history? Tell the class your ideas. Think of some more inventions.

- The first electric light bulb
- The first space rocket
- The first electronic computer
- The first plane
- The first telescope
- The first printing press
- The first round-the-world sailing ships

2 When did it happen?

Inventions in history
Extra practice • WB Ex. 2

Work with a partner.
When do you think the things in Exercise 1 happened?
Put them on the timeline and then compare with other students.

1450, 1534, 1550, 1600, 1880, 1903, 1950, 1961

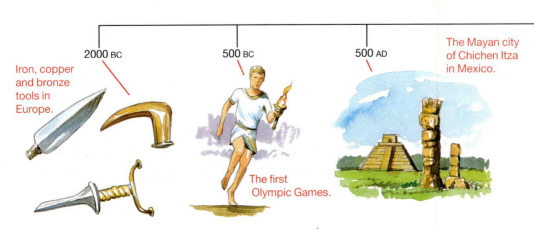

- 2000 BC — Iron, copper and bronze tools in Europe.
- 500 BC — The first Olympic Games.
- 500 AD — The Mayan city of Chichen Itza in Mexico.
- 2000 AD — Cambridge University Press began, the oldest publishing house in the world.

64 Theme C

3 Travel back in time!

Listening

Listen. Travel back in time to check your answers!

4 An important discovery

Reading

4.1 In the mountains

Some years ago, some people discovered something very important in the mountains. You can read a newspaper story about it. These words are in the story. What do you think it tells you?

tourists   a body   snow   police   archaeologists   4,000 years old

4.2 History under the ice

Read the newspaper story. Check if your answers to Exercise 4.1 were correct.

September 22 19

WALKERS FIND MYSTERY BODY IN THE ALPS

LAST THURSDAY, two people discovered a body in the snow on the border of Italy and Austria. Helmut and Erika Simon found an axe, a bow and twelve arrows near the body. The body had boots on, filled with grass. Mr and Mrs Simon called the police immediately. Archaeologists also went to see the body. They think the body is probably over 4,000 years old. Dust from a sandstorm melted the snow over the body.

Archaeologists from Rome and Vienna say that the body can tell us a lot about life thousands of years ago. The body is one of the most important discoveries for a long time. In 1950, archaeologists found some bodies in Denmark. They were also over 4,000 years old.

You can listen to the text on the cassette.

5 Decide ...

Choose an exercise. You can work by yourself, with a partner or in a small group.

Exercise 5.1 checks your vocabulary.
Exercise 5.2 checks your understanding.
Exercise 5.3 practises speaking.

5.1 Check your vocabulary *Vocabulary*

Read the text again. Make a list of the words you don't understand.
Look carefully at the text again.
Can you guess the meaning of the words?
Check the words in the dictionary.
Compare your ideas with others in your class.

> Words I don't understand
> archaeologists
> arrows

5.2 Check your understanding *Comprehension*

Look back at the text. Write your answers to these questions.

1. What did Helmut and Erika Simon find?
2. Where did they find it?
3. What did they do?
4. What do archaeologists think?
5. How did they discover it?
6. What did archaeologists find in 1950?

5.3 Interview Mr and Mrs Simon *Speaking*

Imagine you are a police officer.
You are interviewing Mr or Mrs Simon.
Here are the police notes:

> They found the body at 2.30 p.m. on Monday. They discovered the body on the footpath. First they saw the head and shoulders. They found a small bag. They picked up an axe. They told the police in the village.
>
> Ask! What? When? Where? How? Why?

What questions do you ask?
Interview your partner.

6 Sing a song! Pyramids and dinosaurs

Listen to 'Pyramids and dinosaurs (a long, long, long time ago)' and sing it with your class. The words are on page 155.

7 4,000 years ago they didn't have ... *Writing*

Work with your neighbour.
What things did people have 4,000 years ago, do you think?
What things didn't people have 4,000 years ago? Make a list.

> They had chairs 4,000 years ago. They had clothes 4,000 years ago.
> They didn't have books 4,000 years ago. They didn't have electricity 4,000 years ago.

Compare your list with others in your class.

8 Clues from the past

Finding clues
Extra practice •
WB Ex. 3, 4

8.1 What can you guess?

Archaeologists learned a lot from the body of the Iceman.
What can *you* guess about his life?
Look carefully at the picture of the things near his body.

- Why do you think he was in the mountains?
- Where did his clothes come from?
- Did he cook his food?
- Did he have animals?

Share your ideas with the class.

8.2 Clues, guesses and questions …

When archaeologists find something, they look carefully at it.
They see what clues it gives them, what they can guess about
it, and what questions they can ask.

Can you match the clue, the guess and the question?

We know he had leather boots …	so he probably cooked his food.	But how did he get it from the ground?
We know he had arrows …	so he probably had cows.	But what food did he cook?
We know he had fire …	so he probably had iron.	But what animals did he hunt?
We know he had a metal axe …	so he probably hunted wild animals.	But what did he do with the milk?

9 Decide …

Choose an exercise. You can work by yourself, with a partner or in a small group.

Exercise 9.1 Be a detective!
Exercise 9.2 gives you writing practice.
Exercise 9.3 … Do it yourself!

9.1 Be a detective!

Deducing and writing

Imagine you are an archaeologist.
You found these things under the ice in China.
They are 4,000 years old.
What can you guess about each thing?
What question can you ask?

Write a guess and a question after each fact.

Fact	Guess	Question
We know the person had a lot of horses …	So he or she was probably very rich.	But why did the horses die?
We know the person ate yoghurt …		
We know the person had a lot of wool clothes …		
We know the person made metal …		
We know the person wore a lot of gold jewellery …		

9.2 What did they have 4,000 years ago?

Guided writing

Look at the pictures.
Can you find eight things that were not possible 4,000 years ago?
Write a sentence for each one.
For example:

They didn't have radio 4,000 years ago.

9.3 Do it yourself!

DIY

Decide what you want to do and then ask your teacher.
You can use the *Ideas list* on pages 150–1 to make an exercise for your class *Exercise Box*.

Theme C

10 Your Language Record

Now complete your *Language Record*.

Language Record

Write the meaning of the words in your language. Add the missing examples.

Word	Meaning	Example
a tool		The villagers made tools from stone and metal.
a wheel		People used the wheel to move wood.
a detective		Archaeologists are detectives of the past.
a body		
a train		
steam		At 100°C water makes steam.
snow		
jewellery		People in the past made beautiful gold jewellery.
ice		The ice melted when the climate changed.
metal		People made axes from metal many years ago.
melt		The metal melted in the hot fire.
discover		Archaeologists discover things under the ground.
print		

Choose five more words from the box and write sentences to show their meanings.

> to travel   a boot   a map   to disappear   an axe   a bow   an arrow   dust
> important   a border

Your own notes

....
....

Time to spare? Choose one of these exercises.

1. Write an exercise for your class *Exercise Box* (use the *Ideas list* on pages 150–1) or choose one to do. Check your answers on the back of the paper.
2. Think of some more inventions and discoveries and put them in the right place on the timeline.
3. Imagine that you found the things of some children who lived 4,000 years ago. What things are they? What questions can you ask about their life?

Unit 13   Topic

14 Language focus

Past simple – regular and irregular forms; negative and question forms; reacting

1 Life in the past

Brainstorming; reading

1.1 What do you know about life 4,000 years ago?

Extra practice • WB Ex. 1

Work with your class and brainstorm some answers to these questions:

- Where did people live?
- What did people eat?
- What clothes did they wear?
- Did people travel?
- What did the children do?
- Did people buy and sell things?
- What did people drink?

Life 4,000 years ago

Say it clearly!

/ɪ/ did

You can add some more questions to make a question poster.

1.2 Are you right?

Read the text and check your answers to the questions in Exercise 1.1.

LIFE IN A VILLAGE 4,000 YEARS AGO

Thousands of years ago, there was ice across a lot of the world. When the ice melted and it became warmer, people's lives changed. They began to move from place to place. They didn't live in caves any more. They lived in long houses. They made their houses with small trees and grass.

In those days, the children didn't go to school. They went into the fields and helped with the animals. They had cows, pigs, sheep, goats and dogs, but they didn't have horses, cats or chickens. The women cooked meat and made cheese and butter from milk. They wore wool clothes and leather boots. They didn't have farm machines, but the cows worked with the farmers in the fields.

The people didn't stay in one place. Many people went from village to village. They saw how other people lived. When strangers came to the village they exchanged new ideas. Sometimes they bought things – pots, crops and metal – from each other.

🎧 You can listen to the text on the cassette.

2 'Had', 'went', 'saw' ...

Irregular Past simple
Extra practice •
WB Ex. 1, 5
Extra practice •
TB Ws. 14.1

2.1 Regular and irregular verbs

In Unit 9 you saw some verbs like this:

Dinosaurs liv**ed** millions of years ago. Some of them mov**ed** very quickly.

Verbs that have '-ed' on the end are called 'regular' verbs.
Can you find some more in Exercise 1.2?

There are also 'irregular' verbs in English that don't have '-ed' on the end.
Do you have irregular verbs in your language?

2.2 Some more irregular verbs

Do you know the Past tense of these verbs?

have	They .... cows, pigs and sheep.
go	Many people .... from village to village.
see	They .... how other people lived.

Say it clearly!
/ɔː/ s**aw**, b**ough**t, w**o**re;
/æ/ h**a**d, beg**a**n;
/eɪ/ m**a**de, c**a**me

Look back at the text. Can you find the Past tense of these verbs?
Write an example for each one.

make   begin   come   buy   wear

Look at the list of verbs on page 149.
Can you find the verbs there?

The past form is the same for all persons.

| I You He/She/It We You They | went from place to place. bought things like pots. came to the village. |

2.3 Questions and answers

Do you remember the Iceman from Unit 13?
Match these questions to the correct answers.

1 What clothes did the Iceman wear?
2 What did the Iceman drink?
3 What did he usually eat?
4 What language did the Iceman speak?
5 How did the Iceman make his arrows?

a He usually ate meat and vegetable soup.
b We don't know what language he spoke.
c He made them from wood and he put metal on the end.
d He drank water and milk.
e He wore a wool coat and leather boots. He put grass in his boots.

Can you add some more verbs to the list in Exercise 2.2?
Can you also find them on page 149?

2.4 A trip with your family or friends

You can use the Past simple to talk about something you did.
Think of a time when you went somewhere with your friends or family.
Work in pairs and ask each other questions.

Where did you go?	I went to …
Who did you go with?	I went with …
What did you do there?	I saw/visited/played …
Did you eat anything there?	No, I didn't/Yes, I did. I ate …
Did you drink anything there?	No, I didn't/Yes, I did. I drank …
Did you buy anything there?	No, I didn't/Yes, I did. I bought …

3 Did they do it? No, they didn't!

Past tense negatives and questions

3.1 Past tense questions and negatives

Extra practice •
WB Ex. 2, 3

Extra practice •
TB Ws. 14.2

It's easy to make questions and negatives about the past.
Look at these examples.

MOTHER: Did you give Susan the sweets yesterday?
DAUGHTER: No, I didn't see her.
MOTHER: Oh dear. Did you give them to her sister?
DAUGHTER: No, she didn't come to school.
MOTHER: Well, did you leave them at school?
DAUGHTER: No, I didn't. I gave them to Linda, Susan's friend.
MOTHER: What did she do with them?
DAUGHTER: She put them in her bag, but when she got home …
MOTHER: Yes?
DAUGHTER: … her new dog ate them!

Complete the description of Past tense questions and negatives.
(Think about the order of *the subject, the verb*, and 'did/didn't'.)

To make Past tense questions: To make Past tense negatives:
Did + ... + ... ?   .... + didn't + ... ?

Look back at Exercises 1 and 2.
Can you find some more examples of Past tense
questions and negatives?

Notice that you use 'did' with all persons.

I You He/She/It We You They	didn't	go to school yesterday. see her.	Where	did	I you he/she/it we you they	put it?

3.2 Make a quiz!

Work with a partner. Look back at Units 13 and 14.
Write three questions about life 4,000 years ago. For example:

Did they drive cars? Did they cook their food?

Write three 'true or false' sentences. For example:

They didn't drink milk. True or false?   They didn't live in houses. True or false?

When you are ready, divide the class into two teams.
Take it in turns to ask each other. The first team to get 15 points is the winner!

3.3 SOME MORE PRACTICE A question bag

Work in pairs again. Write some questions to ask other students.

What did you eat for breakfast?   Did you watch television last night?

Put the questions in a bag. Take one and answer with a complete sentence.

---

4 Out and about with English

Reacting
Extra practice • WB Ex. 4

4.1 What can you say?

If you want to ask a friend about last weekend, what questions can you ask?

Did you … ?

4.2 At the weekend

🎧 Listen to Will, Alison, Helen and Nick. Do they ask your questions?

WILL: Hi, Alison, did you have a good weekend?
ALISON: Yes, thanks. I had a great time. I went to the beach with Nick.
HELEN: Brilliant! You lucky thing!
NICK: Yes, it was great. We played handball all day.
ALISON: What did you do, Will?
WILL: I went to see the Mash Boys with Helen.
NICK: Oh, no!
ALISON: Was it good?
NICK: The Mash Boys, good? Never!
HELEN: No, not really. It was very hot and noisy.
ALISON: Oh, bad luck!
HELEN: I wore Ali's sweater.
    Someone put chocolate on it.
ALISON: Oh, no!
WILL: And I bought a Mash Boys cassette.
ALISON: Can I hear it?
WILL: No … because it dropped out of my pocket!
ALISON: That's terrible!

What things do they think were good? What do they say?
What things do they think were bad? What do they say?

4.3 PRACTICE

Work with a partner. Make a conversation about what you did at the weekend.
You can invent any details you like. Look at Exercise 4.2 for ideas.

Did you have a good time in the holidays?

I went …	Oh, brilliant!
I saw …	You lucky thing!
I visited …	Oh no!
I played …	Oh, bad luck!
It was …	That's terrible!

When you are ready, act out your conversation for the class.

5 Do it yourself!

DIY

Look back at Units 13 and 14.
What practice do *you* need? What would *you* like to do?

write an exercise   sing a song   play a game   write a letter   make a puzzle
make a dialogue   discuss something   make a test   read something   … *you decide!*

Plan by yourself or with other students what you will do after Unit 17.
Make some notes in the space in the *Do it yourself* plan on page 82.

6 Your Language Record

Now complete your *Language Record*.

Time to spare? Choose one of these exercises.

1. Write an exercise for your class *Exercise Box* (use the *Ideas list* on pages 150–1) or choose one to do. Check your answers on the back of the paper.
2. Fill the gaps with a question word. Write your answers.

   When   What   Why   How

   Four thousand years ago, ... did they make their houses?
   .... did people wear? .... did the children do? .... did the ice melt?

3. Find eight verbs in Square A. Find the past form in Square B.

Square A

```
S P E A K D R I N K
T J W S T R E J R N
G R T L L A T E I O
E Y J P U T O W S W
T B B C G T Y N R D
C O M E T Y I O G S
J H S E L L P B C W
M A K E W E A R N T
B U Y G H T K P G C
```

Square B

```
S P O K E D R A N K
T J W S T R E J R N
G R T L L A T E I E
O Y J P U T O W S W
T B B C G T Y N R D
C A M E T Y I O G S
J H S O L D P B C W
M A D E W O R E N T
B O U G H T K P G C
```

Choose some more verbs and make a puzzle for other students.

Language Record

Your own phrase book! REACTING

Write the meaning in your language.

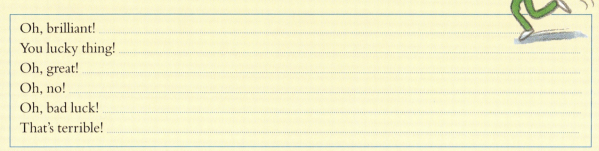

| Oh, brilliant! |
| You lucky thing! |
| Oh, great! |
| Oh, no! |
| Oh, bad luck! |
| That's terrible! |

Irregular verbs
Complete the table.
Fill in the infinitive
or the past form.
Add the missing examples.

Infinitive	Past form	Example
become		The ice melted when it became warmer.
	began	I began school when I was six.
buy		
	came	My friend came to my house yesterday.
drink		I drank a lot of milk yesterday.
	ate	
	got	I got a book for my birthday.
go		
	had	I had a test yesterday.
make		My brother made a cake last night.
put	put	I put your book in your bag.
see		
speak		I spoke to Peter yesterday.
wear	wore	Helen wore a sweater to the concert.

Past tense negatives
Subject + didn't + infinitive …
Write some more examples.
I didn't walk to school yesterday.
I didn't watch TV last night.
I didn't …

Past tense questions
(Question word +) did + subject + infinitive …
Write some more questions.
Where did you go yesterday?
When?
Why?

Revision box 'Was' and 'were'

Write 'was' or 'were' in the gaps.

It .... my birthday yesterday. There .... a lot of presents in my room. My best present .... a trip to the zoo with my friends. All my friends .... very excited. In the zoo, there .... a lot of monkeys. They .... very friendly. There .... a baby monkey. He .... very funny. There .... also two very old monkeys. I think they .... very hungry because they ate my lunch! It .... very late when we came home. I .... very tired.

Unit 14 Language focus

Activity 15 Discoveries for the future

Making a booklet for future historians
Extra practice •
WB Unit 15

In this activity you can make a 'message for the future' to tell people about life today.
When you finish you can bury it!

You will need: pictures of modern things, glue, scissors, paper, pens.

Before your lesson: planning your message

1 Discoveries for the future

Brainstorming

1.1 Our life today

What do you think are the most important things in our life?
What do you think people in the future will want to know about our life today?
Share your ideas with the class.
Think about:

A — Important areas of our life: Machines, Food, school, Clothes

B — Important events of our time

1.2 Plan your message

Work in small groups.

Some of you can work on A …   … and some of you can work on B …

A Important areas of our life	B Important events of our time
Decide what you want to tell people in the future. Decide what pictures and information you need. Decide who can get the pictures and information.	Decide what events you want to tell people in the future. For example, you can tell them about: important events in your country important events in the world important events in sports important discoveries important events in science and so on. Decide what pictures and information you need. Decide who can get the pictures and information.

Bring your information and pictures to your Activity lesson.

Theme C

In your lesson: writing your message for the future

2 Write your message

Sit in your group. Show each other your pictures.
You can put the pictures into groups.
For example, pictures of machines, pictures of people, pictures of important events.
Decide what you can say about each of them.
Decide who in your group can write about each part.

> **Important discoveries**
> A few months ago, some people discovered some pictures in a cave near my town. The pictures are very old and they show some wild animals. People painted them on walls of the cave over 20,000 years ago. They painted them with the juice from fruit and plants.

> **Clothes**
> Here are some of the clothes that we wear today. In the winter it is very cold so we wear thick, heavy clothes like jumpers and coats. Sometimes it is about 0°C. In the summer it is much warmer. Sometimes it is very warm - over 30°C. In the summer we wear light clothes, T-shirts, shorts and sunglasses.

Machines in our life
This is a computer. Computers are very important today. We use them in schools, factories, offices, aeroplanes, trains, at home - everywhere! Computers help us to write, to control machines, to calculate things. Many people also like playing computer games.

> **Important events in Sport**
> This year my country played in the World Cup. The World Cup is a very important football competition every four years. It was very exciting. We played against many different countries and we won 4-2!

While you are writing, help each other with words, spelling and grammar.
Ask your teacher to check your work.

3 Show your work to each other

When you are ready, put your 'messages' on the wall or on your desks.
Go and look at other students' 'messages'.
Perhaps you can give other students more ideas.

Decide what you can do with your message. You can:

- bury it somewhere
- put it in a bottle
- display it in your school
- send it to another school (in your *Parcel of English*)

4 Evaluation

Discuss with the people in your class:

Was it difficult to produce your message? Why? Why not?
Where do you think you need more help?

Would you like to continue your message?
How could you do it better next time?

16 Culture matters The history of the USA

The history of the USA
WB Unit 16:
Help yourself with pronunciation

1 The history of the USA

Brainstorming; reading

1.1 What do you know?

What do you know about the history of the USA?
What famous people in history were from the USA?
What famous events do you know in American history?
How old is the USA?
What people lived there before it became the USA?
Tell the class your ideas.

1.2 Some important events in American history

Work in pairs. Look at the pictures from American history. Can you match them with the descriptions?

- ☐ **Before 1620** Before the English and other Europeans arrived in America, there were already millions of Native Americans there.

- ☐ **1620** These are the first people from England who arrived in America. They left England because of religious problems.

- ☐ **1773** At the 'Boston Tea Party' Americans threw tea into the sea because they did not want to pay tax to the British government.

- ☐ **1776** After a war with Britain, America became an independent country. Americans wrote the Declaration of Independence and designed a new flag – the Stars and Stripes.

- ☐ **1861-65** For four years there was a civil war in the USA between the northern and the southern states. The war was about the slaves who worked on the cotton and sugar farms. The south lost the war, and the government stopped slavery.

78 Theme C

☐ **1876** The Native American tribes lived in America before Europeans arrived. There were many battles between the European settlers and the Native Americans. The Sioux won the Battle of Little Big Horn and kept their land.

☐ **1886** Dr Pemberton made one of the most famous drinks in the world 'to help the brain'.

☐ **1909** An American, Henry Ford, produced the first car: the Model T Ford.

☐ **1963** Martin Luther King, the leader of the black Civil Rights movement in the USA, gave his famous speech, 'I have a dream …'. He wanted black people and white people to be equal at school and at work in the USA.

☐ **1965–75** America fought in Vietnam for ten years to help South Vietnam against North Vietnam. South Vietnam and the Americans lost the war.

☐ **1969** The first people on the moon were three American astronauts: Neil Armstrong, Buzz Aldrin and Ed Collins.

You can hear the texts on the cassette.

2   What is it?   *Listening*

Listen. You can hear some sounds from American history. What do you think they are?

1969 The first people on the moon. ☐

1909 The first Model T Ford. ☐

1965–75 The war in Vietnam. ☐

1886 The most famous drink in the world. ☐

1963 Extract from Martin Luther King's speech, 'I have a dream …'. ☐

1620 The first people from England arrive in America. ☐

Unit 16   Culture matters   79

17 Revision and evaluation

Revision of Units 13–16
Extra practice •
WB Unit 17
Test yourself

1 How well do you know it?

Self-assessment

How well do you think you know the English you learnt in Units 13–16? Put a tick (✓) in the table.

	very well	OK	a little
New words			
Past tense regular and irregular verbs			
Ask questions about the past			
Past tense – negatives			

Now choose some sections to revise and practise.

2 What's the word?

Vocabulary

Look at the pictures. Can you find the words in the word square?

```
A H G T E Y T W H W I J S
M A P H E O I E Y U W H N
J D J K L I C E J D E J O
J F J K W I N F K W J D W
J D J W H E E L W H D H D
J K J D L B O O T Q K N E
K D K O K E N G I N E F H
S T E A M E O J E N W K W
```

Look back through Units 13 and 14. Make a word puzzle for other students to do.

3 All about you

Past tense: regular and irregular verbs

Choose five questions and write your answers.

What time did you go to bed last night?

How did you travel to school today?

What programmes did you see on television last week?

What presents did you get for your last birthday?

What did you eat for dinner last night?

How old were you when you began school?

What did you do last weekend?

What sports did you play last week?

4 The Aztecs

Past simple questions

The Aztecs lived in Mexico a long time before the Spanish went there. Read about how they lived. Write the questions that the text answers.

THE AZTECS

1 When …? The Aztecs lived in Mexico between four and six hundred years ago. They moved there from different parts of South America. In Mexico, they built beautiful cities with big buildings, squares and wide streets.

2 How …? Most of their cities were on islands so they went everywhere by boat. They didn't use horses or wheels for transport.

3 Where …? They built their biggest city on Lake Tezcoco, near today's Mexico City.

4 What …? They had their own Aztec language and they were very advanced in many ways.

5 Did …? They had schools for the children and two calendars – one for their religion and another one to help them plant their crops. Every day, they killed people in the market square to say 'thank you' to their god.

6 What …? Most Aztecs were farmers and fishermen. They ate a lot of fish and hunted wild animals with bows and arrows. They made clay pots to cook their food. They probably did not use money. They bought and sold things in the market with beans. We are not sure if the Aztecs had writing, but they probably did not. When the Spanish arrived in Mexico in 1519, they attacked the Aztecs. Three years later, after a long war, the Spanish took control of Mexico.

7 How …?
8 How …?
9 Did …?
10 When …?

5 Possible or impossible?

Past simple negatives and positives

Are these sentences about the Aztecs possible or impossible? Write your answers.

a The Aztecs had very simple bicycles.

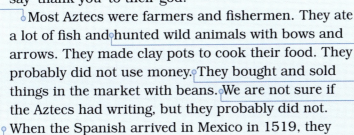
Impossible! They didn't use the wheel.

b There were a lot of Aztecs.
c The cities were very big.
d Some Aztec cities in Mexico are over 1,000 years old.
e The Aztecs spoke Spanish.

f The Aztecs made a lot of things from animal skins.
g Some Aztecs were teachers.
h They wrote letters to each other.
i When the Spanish attacked, the Aztecs used their guns.

Look back at Exercise 4. Were you correct?

6 Looking back at Units 13–16

6.1 Group discussion

Form groups of three or four students.
Decide, with your class, which groups will look at:

Unit 13 *or* Unit 14 *or* Units 15 and 16.

In your group, decide who will report back to the class.
Look through the Units you chose and talk about these questions:

Unit 13	Unit 14	Units 15 and 16
Did you think the topics were interesting? Did you have enough time to do the exercises?	Were the grammar exercises clear? Do you need to practise some more again?	Did you enjoy the activity? What did you learn about the United States?

6.2 Your own ideas

Write down any suggestions you have for future lessons.
Give your paper to your teacher at the end of the lesson.

7 Learning English pronunciation

Work by yourself.
Answer the questions with a tick (√).

	always	often	sometimes	never
1 Do you feel silly when you pronounce a new word?	☐	☐	☐	☐
2 Do you think clear pronunciation is important?	☐	☐	☐	☐
3 Is it difficult to pronounce English?	☐	☐	☐	☐
4 Do you think about pronunciation before you speak?	☐	☐	☐	☐
5 Do you practise pronunciation at home?	☐	☐	☐	☐

Compare your answers with your neighbour and other people in your class. Look at the Workbook Unit 16 for ideas about learning pronunciation.

Open plan

Do it yourself!

See Unit 14 Exercise 5.

Make notes about what you plan to do.

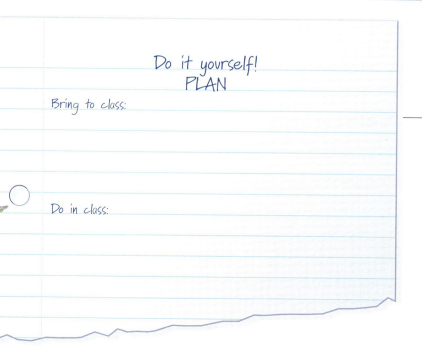

Do it yourself!
PLAN

Bring to class:

Do in class:

Theme D
Below the clouds

Unit ☐

Unit ☐

Unit ☐

Unit ☐

Unit ☐

Take a look at Theme D

Where can you find the pictures? Write the Unit number.
Scan through Units 18 and 19. Can you answer these questions?
– What happened in The Netherlands in January 1995?
– What is a barometer?
– What happened to John?
– Where are Will and Helen?

What can you do in Unit 20?

Topic 18 Climates of the world

The changing world climate; curriculum links with Geography and Environmental Science

1 The climate in your country

Extra practice • WB Ex. 3

How does the climate affect life in your country?
Look at the calendar and brainstorm your ideas with the class.

It's very windy in January. Sometimes planes can't fly.

It's also very cold in January and we can't go swimming.

It's very hot in June. There are a lot of forest fires.

We have a lot of rain in August. There are often floods on the roads.

Say it clearly!
/iː/ eat, /eə/ wear, /ɪə/ year

2 World climates

Reading
Extra practice • WB Ex. 1, 2

Find your country on the map on pages 152–3. What type of climate do you have?
What type of climate do these countries have?

Greenland   Canada   China   Great Britain   Spain   Egypt   India   Brazil

Read the descriptions of the climates again on pages 152–3.
What type of climate does each of these sentences describe?

a It suddenly changes from wet to dry weather.
b It rains all the year and it is usually very warm.
c It is very cold all the time.

IMPORTANT! Do this with an adult!

Make a barometer! An experiment to try at home

A barometer shows when rain is coming.
'High' air pressure = fine weather. 'Low' air pressure = rain (probably).

① Put a candle in water. Put some coins around it. Light the candle. Put a glass jar over it. Watch the water rise.

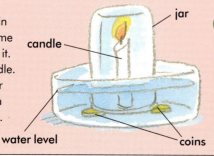

② Check the water level every day. If it goes UP, fine weather is coming. If it goes DOWN, bad weather is coming.

↑ good weather
↓ bad weather

84   Theme D

3 The climate and the way we live

3.1 Climate, houses, food and clothes

Discussion and writing
Extra practice • WB Ex. 4

The climate influences how we live. Work with a partner. Look at the pictures of different places. Can you match them to the traditional houses, food and clothes?

Climates

A The Middle East has a **desert** climate
B Alaska has a **polar** climate
C England has a **cool temperate** climate
D India has a **monsoon** climate

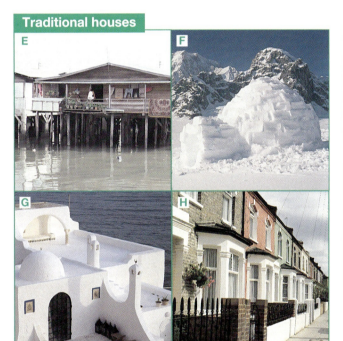

Traditional houses — E, F, G, H

The food they eat

I Raw fish
J Meat and two vegetables
K Curry and rice
L Meat and rice

In each climate, *why* do you think the houses are like that? Why do they eat that food? Why do they wear those clothes? Tell the class your ideas.

> In the Middle East, they paint their houses white to reflect the sun.

> They eat … because …

> They have to wear … because …

What are the houses, food, and clothes like in your country? Why?

The clothes they wear — M, N, O, P

3.2 Write about a climate

Choose a place from Exercise 3.1 or think about your country.
Write about the climate, the houses, the food and the clothes there. For example:

> The Middle East has a desert climate. They paint their houses white to reflect the sun. Not many vegetables grow there, so people eat a lot of meat and rice. They have to wear light clothes and something on their heads because of the heat.

---

4 Decide ...

Choose an exercise. You can work by yourself, with a partner or in a small group.

Exercise 4.1 checks your vocabulary.
Exercise 4.2 checks your understanding.
Exercise 4.3 practises writing.

4.1 What's the word? *Vocabulary*

These words are from the texts on pages 152–3.

> day   above   rise   dry   always   warm

Can you find the *opposites* in the word square? They go across (→), down (↓), and at an angle (↘). Put a word from the square into each sentence.
(You may have to change the word.)

```
N S F E C O L D E W W I J W
I G J U R Y H J W U O E L P
G K B E L O W E W U Q K T E
H T N E V E R F I L T W H A
T J D J E K K D N P Q K O E
H G H R Y T R G E H F A L L
```

1 Hot air rises, but cold air ....
2 In tropical areas, it is never ....
3 In a rainforest it rains every day. The ground is always ....
4 In temperate areas, the temperature does not go .... –3°C.
5 In desert areas, it is very cold at ....
6 In polar areas, the temperature .... rises above 10°C.

Make a puzzle for other students or put it in your class *Exercise Box*.

4.2 Linking sentences *Sentence linking*

Look how these two sentences link together.

> In *the Arctic region* the climate is polar. *There*, they have snow all the year.

In the second sentence 'There' means 'In the Arctic region'. Now look at 1–4. Draw an arrow to show how the second sentence links to the first sentence.

1 In mountain regions there are a lot of trees.
   There, many people live in wooden houses.
2 Countries around the Mediterranean are warm temperate.
   There, the people eat rice or pasta.
3 It often rains heavily in monsoon regions.
   People in those areas build their houses on legs.
4 The rainforests in Brazil are tropical.
   Here it is hot nearly all year round.

Look at the texts on pages 152–3. Find some more sentences with links in the same way.

4.3 Imagine ...   *Writing*

Look at the map on pages 152–3. Choose a place. Imagine that you live there. What do you do every day? What is in your house? What do you eat? How do you use your free time? Describe your life. Give yourself a new name!

Hello, my name is Paco. I live by the sea in Mexico. It's incredibly hot here. There are beautiful birds in the trees and some fantastic insects. It doesn't rain very much here, but when it rains, it rains! The rain is very heavy. In my house, I have ...

5 Disaster from the climate   *Reading*

NATURAL DISASTERS

The climate can make a lot of problems. Look at the pictures and read the texts. What type of climate produced each disaster? (Look at the map on pages 152–3.) Which of the three disasters was the worst?

1 DISASTER IN THE NETHERLANDS

The Netherlands is very flat and part of the country is below the level of the sea. The people there have to make sure that the walls by the sea – the dykes – are very strong. Usually, there is no problem, but in January 1995, it rained and rained for more than two weeks. The water in the canals and rivers rose higher and higher, and thousands of people had to leave their homes because of the danger of floods. They went to other towns and waited until the water level fell again.

2 DISASTER IN FLORIDA, USA

Hurricanes are very strong winds that come from the sea. Warm wet air rises in a spiral and goes faster and faster – over 160 km an hour. In 1992, 'Hurricane Andrew' hit Florida. The people there had to leave their homes and move to other towns and wait. When the hurricane arrived, it killed 15 people and destroyed thousands and thousands of buildings. More than 50,000 people had nowhere to live.

You can hear the texts on the cassette.

Do you have disasters like these in your country?
What do you think we can do to stop disasters happening?
Tell the class your ideas.

3 DISASTER IN AFRICA

Sometimes in desert climates, it does not rain for a very long time. This happened between 1968 and 1974 in The Sahel, in West Africa. The winds changed direction and the area did not receive any rain for six years. Hundreds of thousands of people and nearly half of the animals in the area died because there wasn't enough water. People had to walk many kilometres to find water.

6 Sing a song! Here comes the sun

🎵 Listen to 'Here comes the sun' and sing it with your class. The words are on page 155.

7 Decide …

Choose an exercise. You can work by yourself, with a partner or in a group.
Exercise 7.1 practises writing poems.
Exercise 7.2 practises writing instructions.
Exercise 7.3 … Do it yourself!

7.1 The words in your head *Vocabulary and poems*

What do you think of when you hear or see these words?

sun rain clouds wind summer winter night

Note down your ideas about some of the words. Write down what YOU think of.

- It's hot, and I get tired.
- Long, dry days.
- **Sun**
- The light is bright in the morning.

Use your ideas to write a poem, 'Living in my climate'.

Living in my climate
Where I live it's always hot and dry.
The days are long, and the sun is bright.
After school, I always feel tired.

July comes with heavy rain on the windows.
It makes everything clean.
Ready for the sun,
tomorrow.

7.2 Warning! *Writing*

Read this poster.
It tells you what to do if there is a forest fire.

IMPORTANT INFORMATION

In the FOREST FIRE season
- Always have petrol in the car.
- Have a First Aid kit in the house and car.
- Fill water tanks in the garden with water.
- Cut down trees near the house.

If a FIRE starts ….
- Don't go near the fire.
- Close all the windows in your house.
- Listen to the radio. Follow the instructions on the …

What do people have to do if there are floods, hurricanes, or snowstorms? Write a poster to give information about what to do. Use your imagination!

7.3 Do it yourself! *DIY*

Decide what you want to do and then ask your teacher.
You can use the *Ideas list* on pages 150–1 to make an exercise for your class *Exercise Box*.

8 Your Language Record

Now complete your *Language Record*.

Language Record

Write the meaning of the words in your language. Write the missing examples.

Word	Meaning	Example
climate		England has a very wet climate.
desert		The Sahara is a desert.
fire		
flood		In The Netherlands in 1995, there were floods.
heat (n.)		The sun gives us heat.
kind (n.)		What kind of sports do you like?
level		Parts of The Netherlands are below the level of the sea.
nowhere		After the hurricane, many people had nowhere to live.
above		The temperature in tropical areas is usually above 20°C.
cool		The summers in England are cool.
flat (adj.)		The Netherlands is a very flat country.
heavy		
light (adj.)		In hot countries, people wear light clothes.
heavily		In Switzerland, it often snows heavily.
incredibly		In a desert, it is often incredibly hot.
nearly		Nearly half the animals in The Sahel died.
have to		I have to go to school tomorrow.
make sure		In The Netherlands they have to make sure the dykes are strong.
protect		
receive		The Sahel did not receive any rain for six years.
reflect		White paint helps to reflect the heat.

Choose another word. Add its meaning and an example.

> temperate   polar   tropical   mountain   dry   wet   region

Time to spare? Choose one of these exercises.

1 Write an exercise for your class *Exercise Box* (use the *Ideas list* on pages 150–1) or choose one to do. Check your answers on the back of the paper.
2 Take some of the words from the *Language Record* and make a puzzle.
3 Choose another country in 3.1. Write about the climate there. See 3.2.

Unit 18   Topic   89

19 Language focus

'going to'; 'have to'; making plans; in a café

1 Our changing climate

Discussion; listening

1.1 What is happening to the climate?

Our climate is changing all the time.
Many scientists think that the world is getting warmer.
Why? What things are changing the climate?
Is it important? Tell the class your ideas.

1.2 An international climate conference

🔊 Representatives from over 100 countries are meeting to talk about the environment. Read the text below and then listen to what the news reporter says.

> Hello from the International Climate Conference. There are representatives from over 100 countries here. Yesterday, we heard about plans to help the environment.
> One big problem is the car. The Spanish group, for example, says it is going to ....
> The group from the United States says it is going to ....
> The Italians want to protect their historic cities. They say that many cities are going to ....
> The Germans want to make people use the public transport system more. They plan to ....
> The Japanese group says that Japan is going to ....
> The group from the United Kingdom is going to ....

Work with a partner. One of you can choose List A and the other one List B.
Listen again. Copy and complete the table about each country's plans.

LIST A	Plan
Spain	
Italy	
Japan	

LIST B	Plan
United States	
Germany	
United Kingdom	

Say it clearly!

/gəʊɪŋ tə/ going to

Tell your partner what the countries on your list are going to do:

> The Spanish group is going to …

> The American group is going to …

90 Theme D

2 Talking about the future

'going to' (1)

2.1 What do you say?

How do you talk about the future in your language?

Do you have different ways to talk about the future? What are they?

- Tomorrow, I ...
- Next week, I ...
- Next year, ...
- When I am old, ...

Extra practice •
WB Ex. 1, 3

Extra practice •
TB Ws. 19.1

2.2 Talking about the future in English

In English there are many different ways to talk about the future. One way is to use 'going to'. You can say 'going to' when you want to talk about plans.

How do you say this sentence in your language?

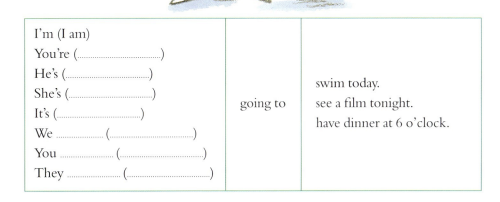

I'm going to play football after school.

2.3 How to form 'going to' sentences

Can you complete the table?
How can you describe 'going to' sentences?

I'm (I am)		swim today.
You're (................)		see a film tonight.
He's (................)	going to	have dinner at 6 o'clock.
She's (................)		
It's (................)		
We .... (................)		
You .... (................)		
They .... (................)		

Negatives and questions are easy!

Are you going to take an umbrella?

They're not going to finish on time.

What are they going to do?

2.4 Guess!

Work in a small group. Write your name on a piece of paper.
Mix up the papers and take one. Think about the person whose name you have.
Write down what you think he or she is going to do:

– after your English lesson   – tomorrow morning
– tonight   – next week

Read your sentences to that person. They can tell you if you are right!

I think (name) is going to ...

Say it clearly!
/ɡəʊɪŋ tə/ going to

Unit 19   Language focus   91

3 What's going to happen?

'going to' (2)

You can also use 'going to' when you think something is *certain* to happen. John woke up late for school this morning. What's going to happen?

John didn't have any breakfast.
He's going to be hungry.

He didn't do his homework.
His teacher is ...

He forgot his coat.

He missed his bus.

He left his football boots at the bus stop.

He lost his money for the bus home.

He isn't going to ...

4 I have to go to school every day

'have to'
Extra practice • WB Ex. 2
Extra practice •
TB Ws. 19.2

4.1 They have to ...

Do you remember these sentences from Unit 18? How do you say them in your language?

In the Middle East, they have to wear light clothes. They have to wear something on their heads.

What does 'have to' mean?

4.2 How to form 'have to' sentences

Can you complete the tables?

I / You (*sing.*) / She/He/It / We / You (*pl.*) / They	have to	eat good food to be healthy. do some exercise every day. go to school on most days.

I / You (*sing.*) / She/He/It / We / You (*pl.*) / They	don't have to	go to school during the holiday. do any homework tonight.

> **Note**
>
> The past of 'have to' is easy:
>
> In 1992 in Florida, thousands of people **had to** leave their homes. In The Sahel, people **had to** walk many kilometres to find water.

4.3 What do you have to do?

How many things do you have to do at home and at school? Work with your neighbour and write a list.

Compare your list with the rest of the class.

At school — I have to arrive at school at 8 a.m.

At home — I have to make my bed.

4.4 Play a game!

Work in a small group. One person chooses a job from the list below.
The others can ask questions to find out which job the person is thinking of.

Say it clearly!

/hæf tə/ have to

The person can only say
'Yes, they do' or 'No, they don't'.
You can also think of some more jobs.

	wear a uniform	work outside	work with people	work at night	sit down a lot
nurses	yes	no	yes	yes	no
police officers	yes	yes	yes	yes	no
taxi drivers	no	no	yes	yes	yes
shop assistants	yes	no	yes	no	no
dentists	no	no	yes	no	no
window cleaners	no	yes	no	no	no
teachers	no	no	yes	no	yes

Do they have to wear a uniform?

Do they have to sit down a lot?

5 Out and about with English

In a café

Extra practice • WB Ex. 3

5.1 What do you say?

If you want to ask for something in a café or restaurant, what do you say?
Look at the menu. What would you like to eat?

5.2 In the school canteen

Listen. Helen and Will are waiting to get their lunch at school.
What is Will going to eat? What is Helen going to eat?
What do they have finally? Who has the best meal, do you think?

HELEN: Well, I'm going to have a hamburger, I think, with lots of chips. And a glass of cola. And some apple pie. Delicious!
WILL: Ugh! I'm going to have some melon and then vegetable pie.
HELEN: Are you going to go to Alison's house after school?
WILL: No, I can't. I have to go to the dentist.
HELEN: We're going to make some things for Pete's party.
ASSISTANT: What would you like?
HELEN: Can I have hamburger and chips, please?
ASSISTANT: I'm sorry. There aren't any hamburgers.
HELEN: Oh, no! OK, vegetable pie, please.
WILL: I'd like melon and vegetable pie, please.
ASSISTANT: Sorry. The pie is finished. She had the last piece.
WILL: Oh, no! What can I have?
ASSISTANT: Spaghetti.
WILL: Oh dear. Melon and spaghetti, please.
ASSISTANT: Would you like a dessert or a drink?
HELEN: Cola and apple pie, please.
WILL: Can I have orange juice, please?
ASSISTANT: Sorry, there's only cola or water.
WILL: What! Water, please.
ASSISTANT: Here you are.
HELEN: That's a healthy meal, Will!

5.3 Now you try it

Work in a small group. Imagine that you are in a café.
One of you is the waiter. Look at the menu (or write a new menu).
Talk about what you are going to have. Talk about what you are going to do later.
Ask the waiter for your food.

What are you going to have?	I'd like …
What are you going to do?	Can I have … ?
I have to …	What would you like?
	I'm sorry. There aren't any …

When you are ready, act out your conversation for the class.

6 Do it yourself!

DIY

Look back at Units 18 and 19. What practice do *you* need? What would *you* like to do?

write an exercise	sing a song	play a game	write a letter	make a puzzle
make a dialogue	discuss something	make a test	read something	… *you decide!*

Plan by yourself or with other students what you will do after Unit 22.
Make some notes in the space in the *Do it yourself* plan on page 102.

7 Your Language Record

Now complete your *Language Record*.

Time to spare? Choose one of these exercises.

1 Write an exercise for your class *Exercise Box* (use the *Ideas list* on pages 150–1) or choose one to do. Check your answers on the back of the paper.
2 What do children *have to* do? What do adults *have to* do?

The life of a child
They have to go to school.
They have to do homework.
They have to …

The life of an adult
They have to go to work.
They have to look after children.
They have to …

Who has the best life – children or adults?
3 Is every morning the same in your house? Write down what you think someone in your house is going to do tomorrow morning. For example:

Tomorrow morning, my brother is going to get up. He's going to go to the bathroom. First, he's going to clean his teeth …

Tomorrow, see if you are right!

Language Record

Your own phrase book! IN A CAFÉ

Add more phrases. Write the meaning in your language.

> What are you going to have? ....
> I'm going to have … ....
> What would you like? ....
> I'd like … ....
> Can I have …? ....
> ....

Going to   Write some examples.

On Sunday afternoon I am *going to* see a film at the cinema. On Monday, I .... On ...., I ....
On .... , my friend ....

Complete the questions.
My train arrives at 2 o'clock. .... to meet me?
He's running towards the goal. .... to score a goal?
She's good at all the science subjects. .... to be a doctor?

Have to   Complete the tables.

| I / You (sing.) / She/He/It / We / You (pl.) / They | .... have to .... | do some homework. get up early. |

| I / You (sing.) / She/He/It / We / You (pl.) / They | .... don't have to .... | go there today. finish this today. |

Revision box 'Much' and 'many'

Write 'much' or 'many' in the gaps.

HELEN: How .... homework have you got tonight?
WILL: I don't know how .... maths exercises! Have you got .... homework?
HELEN: No, not ...., I didn't have .... lessons today. We went to the museum.
WILL: Great! Did you buy anything? How .... money did you spend?
HELEN: Well, I didn't buy .... things. Look, I bought these old coins.
WILL: Wow! How .... did they cost?
HELEN: Not .... They're not real, Will. They're only copies.
WILL: See what the bus driver thinks!

Activity 20 A new book of world climates

Making a book cover
Extra practice • WB Unit 20

In this Unit, you can make a cover for a book about the world's climates. You will need some large pieces of paper or card (A4), magazine pictures and coloured pens ... and your imagination!

Before your lesson: a book and its cover

1 A new book about the world and its climates

Imagine ... a new book about the world's climates. What do you think is in it?
What pictures does it have? What does it tell you about the world?
What do you think the chapters are about? Tell the class your ideas.
(Look back at Units 18 and 19.)

A book about the world's climates.
- Pictures of deserts.
- About the sun.
- How people live in...

2 Discuss and decide

Work in a small group. Imagine that you have to make the cover for the new book.
What can you put on it? In your group discuss:

- what pictures you can put on the front
- what titles the book can have
- what you can write on the back of the book
  (look at the back of this book for ideas!)

Note: the new book is exactly the same size as your English book!

3 Collect the pictures

In your group, decide who can collect which pictures. You can use:

  magazine pictures   photographs   drawings   other pictures

Bring lots of pictures to your Activity lesson. You can share your pictures.

In your lesson: making the book cover

4 Make the front of your book cover

Sit with your group. Show each other the pictures you have. Decide with the group which pictures *you* can put on the front of *your* book. Decide where you can put the title. Decide where you can put the name of the author (you!).

Glue the pictures, write the title and names, and colour the cover. Use one piece of paper for the front of the book and another piece for the back of the book.

5 Make the back of your cover

With your group, make notes about what you want to say on the back of the book.

Now write the back cover of your book. Check spellings, grammar, and words with each other. When you have finished, read your work and check it again.

A new book about the climate
- exciting and beautiful
- lots of interesting information
- fantastic pictures
- tells you about…

OUR LIVING EARTH
This new book is about the world's climates today. It has over 400 beautiful pictures from all over the world and has important and useful information about many countries.
The book has eight chapters:
- Tropical climates – read about the rainforests in Brazil. Learn about the people who live there.
- Polar climates. Brrrr! Learn about igloos and Eskimos. Read about the way they live and what they eat.
- Mountain climates…

Copy your work onto the paper and colour the back cover.

6 Look at other book covers

Put your book covers on the wall or on your desk. Look at other student's work. You can glue the papers onto card and use them for your English work.

7 Evaluation

Discuss these questions with your class.

- Did you work well in your group?
- Was it difficult to make the book covers?
- Did you enjoy making them?
- Was it difficult to write?
- How can you do it better next time?

21 Culture matters   An outdoor life

Leisure activities in the UK and in your country
WB Unit 21:
Help yourself with grammar

1 Leisure activities in your country

Discussion

What activities do people do outdoors in your country? When do they do them? Look at the pictures in this Unit. Can you do the same activities in your country? Where?

Cycling

2 Leisure activities in the United Kingdom

Discussion; listening

2.1 An activity for every season

In the UK, there are many different outdoor activities that you can do. Look at the pictures. Which activities do you think people do all the year? When do you think they do the other activities?

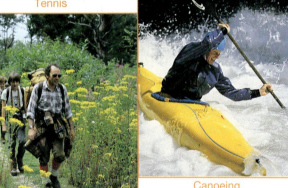

Tennis

Canoeing

Rock climbing

Fishing

Walking

Cricket

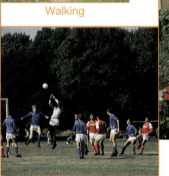

Gardening

Football

Do you do any of these activities?
Which activities would you like to do?
Tell the class what you think.

2.2 The Blake family

🔊 The Blake family has a very active life. They enjoy lots of different outdoor activities. Listen. Fill in the chart with details of what they do and when.

	Activity	When do they do it?	Activity	When do they do it?
Mrs Blake				
Mr Blake				
Tim				
Tara				

3 The Youth Hostels Association (YHA) *Reading*

3.1 What is the YHA?

'Hostelling' is very popular in Britain. Read about the Youth Hostels Association and what it offers. How old do you have to be to use a youth hostel?
Is it expensive to stay in a hostel?

🎧 You can listen to the text on the cassette.

3.2 A youth hostel holiday

Welcome to the YHA!

The Youth Hostels Association offers hostels all over the country.

It costs very little to become a member and you can then stay in any youth hostel in the world.

Youth hostels are places for young people of any age to stay. They do not cost very much and they are clean and comfortable. Many youth hostels are in beautiful countryside with lots of activities to do nearby. While you are at a hostel, you can go walking, climbing, canoeing, sailing …
the choice is yours!

Youth hostels in England and Wales

Tara went with a group from her school to a youth hostel in the Lake District in Northern England. Read Tara's letter to her parents. How many different activities did Tara do? On what day did she write the letter?

> July 23rd
>
> Dear Mum and Dad
> This place is brilliant! There are so many exciting things to do here. On our first day we went canoeing on the lake (look at the photograph!). We also learned how to make a raft. The next day, we went for a long walk in the forest. We had to use a map to find our way to the next village. It was really difficult! On Tuesday, some people went bird-watching but I decided to go and build a tree house with some friends. Tomorrow, we're going to climb the rocks at Coniston and then on Friday we're going to have a big fire and cook our own food. It's really exciting!
> See you on Saturday!
> Love
> Tara

4 Across cultures

Do you have youth hostels in your country?
Find out from your family and friends what outdoor activities you can do in your area.

22 Revision and evaluation

Revision of Units 18–21
Extra practice •
WB Unit 22

1 How well do you know it?
Self-assessment

How well do you think you know the English you learnt in Units 18–21? Put a tick (√) in the table.

	very well	OK	a little
New vocabulary			
Talk about different climates			
Talk about what's going to happen			
Talk about things people have to do			

2 Test yourself!
A test

Work with your neighbour and do this short test.

TEST YOURSELF!

A New vocabulary
Vocabulary

Read the sentences and fill in the gaps. Find the words in the puzzle.

1 The Sahara is a d................... .
2 Don't touch! It's hot! It can b................... you!
3 The temperature in polar areas is never a................... 10°C.
4 A hurricane can d................... houses.
5 A lot of The Netherlands is below the l................... of the sea.
6 In countries with a monsoon climate, it rains very h................... .
7 What k................... of music do you like?
8 It's very w................... in here. Can we open a window?
9 The Netherlands is a very f................... country.
10 I don't h................... to go to school tomorrow.

```
H E A V I L Y H K U H L
H D E S E R T A F A T E
F L A T O I W P Q A R V
X K B U R N D H O B J E
K I N D J W U A J O M L
K D H A V E N M F V P V
D E S T R O Y J Q E Q B
H F J E U W T W A R M N
```

B Talk about different climates (look at the map on pages 152–3)
Climates

Are these sentences true or false?

1 Brazil has a monsoon climate.
2 They receive very little rain in tundra areas.
3 People in England paint their houses white because of the heat.
4 France has a tropical climate.
5 In desert areas, it is warm at night.
6 In tropical areas, it changes very quickly from a wet to a dry season.
7 The climate of your country is warm temperate.
8 Switzerland has a mountain climate.

C Talk about what's going to happen   'going to'

Complete the sentences. Use 'going to'.

> I've got a new bicycle. I'm going to ride to school.

1 I've got a cinema ticket …
2 They've got a new football …
3 We've got some money …
4 It's her birthday tomorrow. She's …
5 His father has got a new job. He's …

D Talk about what people have to do   'have to'

Look at Simon's diary.
Write about what he
has to do every day.

On Monday at 4pm Simon has to go to the dentist …

Monday	Thursday
4pm: dentist.	6pm: Anne's party.
Tuesday	Friday
7pm: guitar lesson.	Tidy my bedroom.
Wednesday	Saturday
1.30: basketball practice.	Buy present for grandmother.
	Sunday
	3pm: Swimming with Uncle Jack.

On Monday at 4pm Simon has to go to the dentist …

Check your answers on page 142. Look back at Exercise 1. Were you right?

---

3 Write your own test!   *Write a test*

Work in small groups.
Look back at Units 18–21 and write part of a test for your class.
Look at the test in Exercise 2 for ideas.
Tell your teacher which part you are doing.

A New vocabulary.
   Make a word puzzle and write some sentences with gaps for clues.

B Talk about different climates.
   Write some true/false sentences about different climates.

C Talk about what's going to happen.
   Write or draw some situations.

D Talk about things you have to do.
   Write a page of someone's diary, or draw a picture of things they have to do.

Check your work and write the answers to your part of the test.
Give the test to your teacher to check and to put together for your class.

4 Looking back at Units 18–21

Evaluation

4.1 Group discussion

Form groups of three or four students.
Decide, with your class, which groups will look at:

Unit 18 *or* Unit 19 *or* Units 20 and 21.

In your group, decide who will report back to the class.
Look through the Units you chose and talk about these questions:

Unit 18	Unit 19	Units 20 and 21
Did you think the topics were interesting? Did you have enough time to do the exercises?	Were the grammar exercises clear? Do you need to practise some more again?	Did you enjoy the activity? What did you learn about the climate of the UK?

4.2 Your own ideas

Write down any suggestions you have for future lessons.
Give your paper to your teacher at the end of the lesson.

5 Learning English grammar

Work by yourself.
Answer the questions with a tick (√).

		always	often	sometimes	never
1	Do you think you have problems with grammar?	☐	☐	☐	☐
2	Do you like learning grammar?	☐	☐	☐	☐
3	Do you think grammar is important?	☐	☐	☐	☐
4	Do you think grammar is difficult?	☐	☐	☐	☐
5	Do you practise grammar at home?	☐	☐	☐	☐

Compare your answers with your neighbour and other people in your class. Look at the Workbook Unit 21 for ideas about learning grammar.

Open plan

Do it yourself!

See Unit 19 Exercise 6.

Make notes about what you plan to do.

Do it yourself!
PLAN

Bring to class:

Do in class:

Topic 23 The global village

Trade and where goods come from; curriculum links with Geography and Economics

1 In the shops

Discussion
Extra practice • WB Ex. 1

1.1 The things you buy

Look at the pictures. Do you ever buy these things?
Which cassettes, magazines, games, etc. do you like most?
Tell the class what you think.

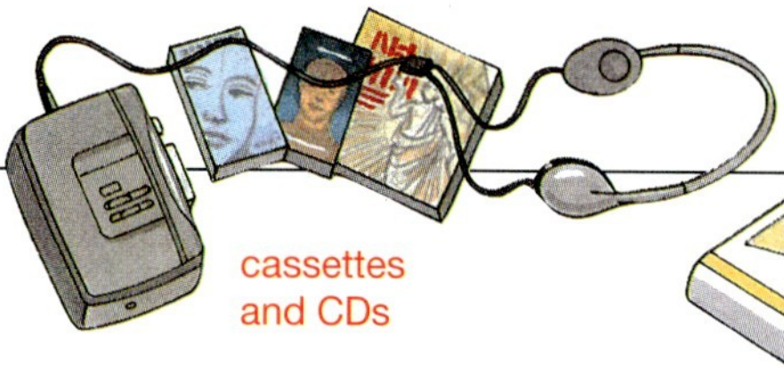

cassettes and CDs

chocolate and sweets

fizzy drinks

snacks

computer games

posters

books and magazines

clothes

sports shoes

Say it clearly!

/s/ drink**s**, book**s**
/z/ clothe**s**, shoe**s**

1.2 What are they made from?

Work with a partner. Look back at the things in Exercise 1.1.
What are they made from? Where does the raw material come from?

2 Primary products from all over the world

Discussion and reading
Extra practice •
WB Exs. 2–4

2.1 What are primary products?

Primary products are raw materials … … and agricultural products.

copper

iron

aluminium

rubber

wheat

leather

cotton

cocoa

sugar

Primary products are very important.
With them, we make many other things.
What things do we make with the primary products
in the pictures? Tell the class your ideas.

2.2 Who exports them?

Do you know where the things in Exercise 2.1 come from? Work with your neighbour and write the names of the primary products under the correct parts of the world.

Latin America (e.g. Mexico, Brazil, Chile, Argentina)	North America (e.g. USA, Canada)	Australasia (e.g. Australia, New Zealand)
Asia (e.g. India, Pakistan)	Europe (e.g. Britain, France, Italy)	Africa (e.g. Kenya, Tanzania, Guinea)

2.3 Who imports them?

Many countries import primary products and manufacture things with them. Read the texts and match them to the products.

A Svensons of Sweden made this telephone. The copper for the wire came from Chile, in South America.

B Sainco supermarket in France made this cake. The wheat for the flour came from Canada. The sugar came from India.

C Thyssen in Belgium made these chocolates. The cocoa beans came from West Africa.

D Peroni of Italy made these shoes. The leather came from Argentina.

E González of Spain made this frying pan. The aluminium came from Guinea, in Africa.

F Sports Wear in England made this T-Shirt. The cotton came from Pakistan.

G Bens in the United States made this car. The rubber for the tyres came from Malaysia in South-East Asia.

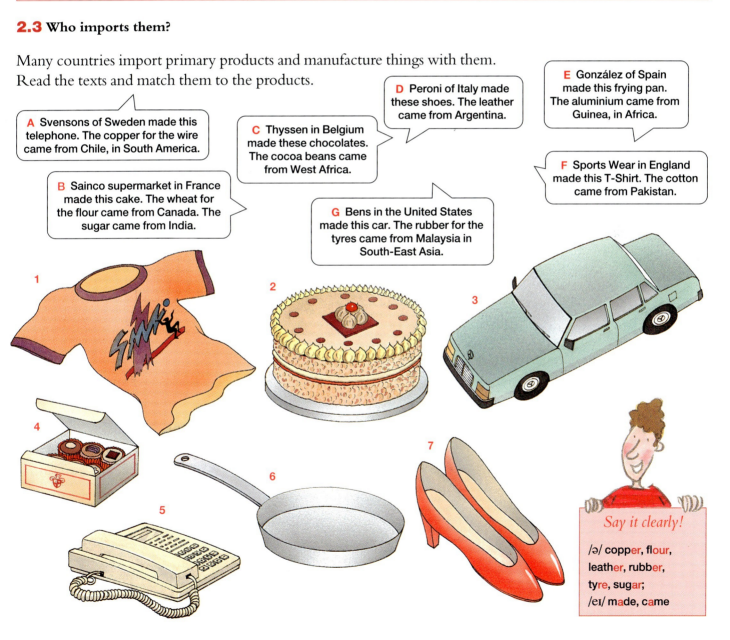

Say it clearly!

/ə/ copper, flour, leather, rubber, tyre, sugar;
/eɪ/ made, came

3 Play a game! International trade

A game

Choose twelve things from Exercise 1.1 and Exercise 2.3 (or from your own ideas) and write them on the bingo card. Your teacher is going to say some primary products. If you have something *made from the primary product*, cross it off. When you have crossed nine things off, shout 'Bingo!'

4 Decide …

Choose an exercise. You can work by yourself, with a partner or in a small group.

Exercise 4.1 checks your vocabulary.
Exercise 4.2 gives you guided writing practice.
Exercise 4.3 gives you free writing practice about an advertisement.

4.1 Odd one out

Vocabulary

In each line one word is different. Choose the different word. Say why.

1. bus   car   train   <u>airport</u>
2. gas   oil   money   coal
3. magazines   games   books   newspapers
4. Brazil   India   copper   Mexico
5. jeans   shoes   T-shirts   clothes
6. cake   bread   wheat   biscuits
7. make   expand   produce   manufacture
8. sugar   bananas   cars   apples
9. sea   river   forest   lake
10. iron   cocoa   copper   aluminium
11. sugar   leather   people   wheat
12. radio   cotton   television   computer

(Crossword puzzle with answers: 'import' and 'export')

Write the words in the right place (down ↓) in the puzzle. Write another 'odd one out' puzzle. You can write clues about names of foods, fruits, places, metals, sports, inventions … look at Units 1–22 for ideas.

4.2 An international birthday

Guided writing

It's someone's birthday!
Look at the cake, the box, and the balloons.
What are they made from?
Where do the primary products come from?
Write about each thing.

Chocolate is made from cocoa beans. The cocoa beans came from West Africa.

The sugar came from …

4.3 Buy it!

Choose one of the things in Exercise 2.3 (or think of another product). Imagine that you want to sell it. Draw a picture, give it a name, and write a short advertisement. For example:

Free writing

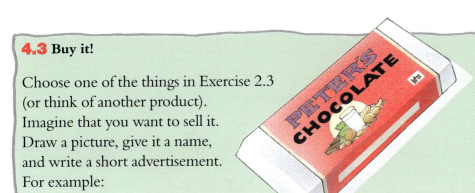

It's delicious! It's the best! It's in the shops now! Peter's chocolate is the best chocolate that you can buy. It's made from the best cocoa beans from Africa. Enjoy the taste of Peter's chocolate today!

---

5 Across the world

Discussion and reading

5.1 Companies from across the world

Do you know these logos? Can you match them to the correct picture? What country do the companies come from?

1 Levi's
2 McDonald's
3 VW
4 NIKE
5 PEPSI
6 SONY

Companies that work in many different countries are called 'multinationals'. Often, multinationals have their head offices in Europe, North America or Japan and their factories in other countries. Can you think of the names of any more multinationals?

5.2 Some points of view

Some people think that multinationals are good for the countries where they have their factories. Other people think that they are bad.

Read these sentences. How much do you understand?
Underline in red the sentences you understand completely.
Underline in blue the sentences where you can guess the meaning.
Underline in green the sentences you don't understand.

A The local people sometimes work in dangerous conditions.

B The multinationals bring a lot of money to the country.

C The multinationals bring education to local people.

D Multinationals bring a lot of jobs to the country.

E Multinationals send the money that they make to their own country.

F Multinationals give the best jobs to foreigners.

G Multinationals do not pay high wages to local people.

H Multinationals make us part of a 'global village'.

I The multinational companies build new roads, airports or railways.

J The multinational companies make things which people want to buy.

K Local factories can make things for the multinational companies.

L The multinationals have modern technology.

Work with a partner and compare your colours. Help each other understand the difficult sentences. Look in your dictionary, or ask your teacher if you need help!

Say it clearly!

/ʃ/ national, education, condition

5.3 Good or bad?

Which sentences in Exercise 5.2 say multinationals are good?
Which say they are bad? Make two lists.

Good   Bad

6 Sing a song! Big money

📼 Listen to 'Big money' and sing it with your class.
The words are on page 156.

7 Decide …

Vocabulary

Choose an exercise. You can work by yourself, with a partner or in a small group.

Exercise 7.1 practises vocabulary.
Exercise 7.2 practises writing.
Exercise 7.3 … Do it yourself!

7.1 A word map   *Vocabulary*

Choose one of the things in Exercise 2.3 or 5.1. What words do you know that connect to it? What words do you think of? Make a word map of the words in your head. For example:

Sports — Fast — Types — Racing — Wheels — Expensive — Problems — Noisy — Dirty — Motor car — Tyres — People — Travel — Planes — Rockets — Trains

7.2 What's your favourite?   *Writing*

Look at the pictures of the things in this Unit again. Choose three or four and write about your favourite magazine, cassette or CD, game, etc. For example:

My favourite magazine is 'Animal Magic'. It is very interesting. It always has a lot of information. Every week, it has a free poster. My favourite is …

7.3 Do it yourself!   *DIY*

Decide what you want to do and then ask your teacher.
You can use the *Ideas list* on pages 150–1 to make an exercise for your class *Exercise Box*.

8 Your Language Record

Now complete your *Language Record*.

Language Record

Write the meaning of the words in your language.
Write the missing examples. Add some more words.

Word	Meaning	Example
made		Books are made from paper.
copper		Electric wires are made from copper.
iron		Iron is a very important metal.
aluminium		Aluminium comes from bauxite.
cocoa		Chocolate is made from cocoa beans.
cotton		Shirts are often made from cotton.
rubber		Car tyres are made from rubber.
leather		My shoes are made from leather.
wheat		
flour		
wire		There are many wires in a telephone.
bean		
primary product		Cotton, iron, and leather are primary products.
raw material		Iron, diamonds, and copper are raw materials.
tyre		A car usually has four tyres.
foreigner		
local		
wages		Many people get very low wages.
education		A good education is very important.
conditions		Many people work in bad conditions.
manufacture		They manufacture cars in Brazil.
import (v.)		
export (v.)		

Time to spare? Choose one of these exercises.

1 Write an exercise for your class *Exercise Box* (use the *Ideas list* on pages 150–1) or choose one to do. Check your answers on the back of the paper.
2 Copy eight sentences from Exercise 5.2 but leave out the verb. Ask your neighbour if he/she can fill in the verb.
3 Write another 'odd one out' puzzle like the one in Exercise 4.1, or another advertisement like the one in Exercise 4.3.

24 Language focus

Modals – 'could', 'would'; 'enough'; prepositions of place; asking the way (1)

1 On the road

Listening and reading

🔊 Ken is a lorry driver in England. He takes containers to and from airports, ferries, railway stations and factories. Listen. Ken's boss is planning trips for next week.

Listen to their conversation. First, draw a line on the map to show where Ken has to go.

Listen again and complete Ken's worksheet.

	Morning	Afternoon
Mon	Portsmouth	
Tues		
Wed		
Thurs		
Fri		

2 'Could you …?'

'could': making a request; speaking

2.1 Making a request

Ken's boss asked him to go to different places like this:

- Could you pick up some washing machines?
- Could you collect some pencils in Bristol?
- Could you drive back to London?

How do you say the same things in your language?

Extra practice • WB Ex. 1
Extra practice • TB Ws. 24.1

Say it clearly!

/kəd juː/ could you

2.2 Who says what?

Match the sentences to the pictures.

1. Could you open your suitcase, please?
2. Could you answer the phone, Tim?
3. Could you finish this exercise for Friday, please?
4. Could you lend me your new cassette tonight?
5. Could you turn the music down, please?
6. Could you tell me where Smith's supermarket is, please?

Check your answers with your partner. What can the people in the pictures answer?

You can listen to the dialogues on the cassette.

2.3 Play a game! What do you want?

Work in a small group (or with the whole class).
Mime a request. The other students have to guess what you are asking. For example:

Could you lend me your pen?

The person who guesses correctly has the next turn. You can use these verbs:

lend show give open help bring carry write put

---

3 'Would you like ...?'

'would': making an offer

Extra practice • WB Ex. 2
Extra practice •
TB Ws. 24.1

3.1 Making an offer

Ken's boss asks him: Would you like to have a rest on Friday?

Here are some more examples:

Would you like a sandwich?
No, thanks. I'm not hungry.

Would you like to go to the cinema?
Yes, please. I love watching films!

How do you say these sentences in your language?

3.2 Make an offer

Work with a partner. Look at the pictures and offer each other something.
Answer with a complete sentence.

4 Have you got enough time?

'enough'
Extra practice • WB Ex. 3

4.1 'Enough' in your language

How do you say these sentences in your language?

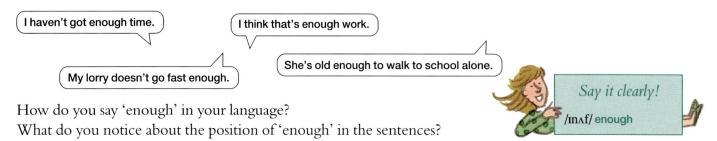

- I haven't got enough time.
- I think that's enough work.
- My lorry doesn't go fast enough.
- She's old enough to walk to school alone.

Say it clearly! /ɪnʌf/ enough

How do you say 'enough' in your language?
What do you notice about the position of 'enough' in the sentences?

4.2 Where do you use 'enough'?

Do you remember what a **noun** and an **adjective** are?
Look at the sentences in Exercise 4.1 again and find the nouns and adjectives.

Where do you use 'enough' – **before** or **after** adjectives and nouns?
Share your ideas with the class.

4.3 What are they saying?

Write a sentence for each picture. Use 'enough'.

5 Out and about with English

Asking the way (1)
Extra practice • WB Ex. 5
Extra practice •
TB Ws. 24.2

5.1 Around town

Look at this map. Can you write the correct name on each place? For each one, make a list of what you can do or buy there.

a baker's
bread
cakes
biscuits

baker's   hospital   post office
newsagent's   bank   supermarket
train station   bus station
doctor's   chemist's

Compare your map and lists with other students in the class.

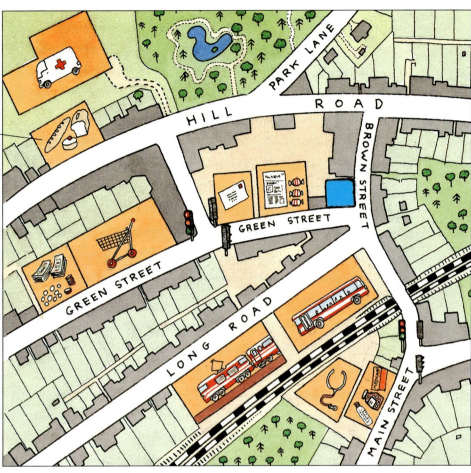

5.2 Can you tell me where it is?

Helen and Will are on holiday. They want to do some shopping. This is their shopping list. Where do you think they want to go?

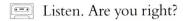 Listen. Are you right?

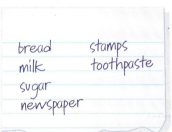

bread   stamps
milk   toothpaste
sugar
newspaper

HELEN: OK. Now, where do we have to go?
WILL: Well, we can get the milk and sugar in a supermarket. And the bread.
HELEN: Let's get the bread in a baker's. It's better.
WILL: OK. We need a newsagent's, and the post office for the stamps.
HELEN: What about the toothpaste?
WILL: In a chemist's, or in the supermarket. Let's go to a supermarket first. Let's ask someone.
WILL: Excuse me, where can we find a supermarket?
WOMAN: A supermarket? Well, I think the nearest supermarket is in Green Street, next to the bank.
WILL: Thanks.
HELEN: This is Green Street. I can't see a supermarket.
WILL: Let's ask this man.
HELEN: Excuse me, do you know where the supermarket is?

MAN: Sorry, I don't know this town.
HELEN: Oh, thanks. Let's ask this woman.
WILL: Excuse me. We're lost. Could you tell us where there is a supermarket?
WOMAN: Yes, there's one in front of you!
HELEN: Oh yes! Thank you.
WILL: Helen, look at that poster! There's a Mash Boys concert tomorrow!
HELEN: Let's get some tickets! I wonder where the concert hall is?
WILL: Well, we can ask someone.
HELEN: Oh no! Not again.

5.3 Now you try it

Work in pairs. Look at the map in Exercise 5.1 again. Ask each other where each place is.

— Excuse me. Do you know where the post office is?
— Yes, it's in Green Street, next to the newsagent's.

Excuse me. Could you tell me where … is?   Excuse me. Where can I find …?
next to   in front of   behind   on the left of   on the right of

Act out a conversation for the class.

6 Do it yourself!

DIY

Look back at Units 23 and 24. What practice do *you* need? What would *you* like to do?

write an exercise   sing a song   play a game   write a letter   make a puzzle
make a dialogue   discuss something   make a test   read something   … *you decide!*

Plan by yourself or with other students what you will do after Unit 27.
Make some notes in the space in the *Do it yourself* plan on page 122.

7 Your Language Record

Now complete your *Language Record*.

Time to spare? Choose one of these exercises.

1 Write an exercise for your class *Exercise Box* (use the *Ideas list* on pages 150–1) or choose one to do. Check your answers on the back of the paper.
2 What do your parents ask you to do at home? What do your teachers ask you to do at school? Make a list of their requests.   Could you …?
3 Look at the map in Exercise 5.1 again. Write a dialogue in which a person is trying to find a chemist's.

114   Theme E

Language Record

Your own phrase book! ASKING THE WAY (1)

Add more phrases. Write the meaning in your language.

> Excuse me, where is the post office? ....
> Could you tell me where the post office is, please? ....
> Where can I find the post office? ....
> I'm lost. Do you know where the post office is? ....
> ....
> ....

Write the meaning in your language.

'enough' + noun:
I don't have enough money. ....

adjective + 'enough':
I'm not rich enough to buy a car. ....

'could' to ask someone to do something:
Could you open the window, please? ....

'would' to offer someone something:
Would you like some orange juice? ....

Write a sentence.

Offer someone something to eat. ....
Ask someone to buy some sweets for you. ....

Revision box The irregular Past simple

1. **Regular and irregular verbs**
   To make the past form of regular verbs you add '-ed' (play/played, talk/talked). Other verbs are 'irregular' (eat/ate, go/went). Can you remember any irregular past verbs? Write them down.

2. **Play a game in a small group!**
   First draw a picture of a person with ears, eyes, mouth, hands and feet. Draw an arrow to each part of the body and write a verb next to it (e.g. head – think – thought: hands – hold – held). Say a sentence with that verb, e.g. 'Yesterday I thought I was an astronaut'. Point to another part of the body. Another student continues the story with a sentence from that part of the body. Say your story round the class until all the parts of the body are finished.

3. **Your day yesterday**
   Write four true sentences about your day yesterday, and four false sentences. Give them to your neighbour. Can they guess which ones are true and which ones are false? Use the past tense of some of these verbs: buy, come, drink, go, have, make, put, see, speak, wear.

Activity 25 Come to see us!

Making a tourist leaflet about your area

Extra practice • WB Unit 25

In this Unit, you can make a tourist leaflet or poster about the area where you live. You will need: paper, glue, pens and crayons, plus postcards of your area, photographs and pictures.

Before your lesson: planning

1 The South West of England

The pictures in this Unit all come from the South West of England. Look carefully at them and discuss these questions with your class.

- What kind of climate does the South West have?
- What kind of jobs do the people there do?
- What sports do they do?
- What can tourists do there?

2 The South West – a tourist leaflet

Were you right? Read about the South West. Match the texts to the pictures.

Welcome to the South West!

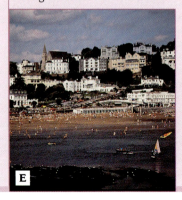

1 GEOGRAPHY
The South West is the warmest part of the UK. There are some hills in the north near Bristol, but the rest of the area has some very flat parts which are below the sea. There are beaches on both sides of the area.

2 CLIMATE
The climate here is temperate. The winters are warmer than other parts of the UK. The summers are usually warmer and drier than other areas. Some summer days are very hot. It sometimes rains a lot in the spring. It is often very windy in the winter.

3 FARMING
There are a lot of farms in the South West. Most of the farms are very big and have 500 cows or 2,500 pigs or even 5,000 hens. Many farms grow apples and other kinds of fruit. Cheese and cream are the specialities of the area.

4 INDUSTRIES
There are many different kinds of industries in the South West. In Bristol, many people work in factories which make aeroplanes. In other towns many people work in small factories which make shoes. There are also many small factories which make cheese and butter and yoghurt.

5 ALL ABOUT THE PEOPLE
Many of the families who live in the South West have lived here for a long time. Their grandfathers and grandmothers were farmers on the same land. In their free time they like fishing and walking. Many people like cycling because the land is very flat in many parts of the area.

You can listen to the texts on the cassette.

116 Theme E

3 Your own leaflet

You can make a leaflet about where you live. Discuss your ideas with your class.
What can you say about:

- the geography there?
- your climate?
- the industries?
- the farms?
- the transport?
- what people do?

Decide what pictures you can get about your area. Decide who can get them.

In your lesson: making a leaflet

4 Making the leaflet

Work in a group to make a leaflet. Look at the pictures that you have.
Decide who can write about each topic.

Geography
Is your area near the sea?
Is your area flat or hilly?
Are there a lot of rivers and lakes?

Industries
Are there any big factories in your area?
What do they make?
What other industries are there?

The climate
What type of climate do you have?
Do you have different seasons?
What are they like?
Is it a nice area to live in?

The people in your area
How many people live in your area?
What do they do?
What do they do in their free time?
Where do they live?

Farming
Is there a lot of farming in your area?
Do many people work on farms?
What types of farms are there?

While you are working, help each other with words, spelling and grammar.
Draw a map of your area. Write about some of the important places.
Stick your pictures into your leaflet.

When you are ready, put your leaflet on the wall or on your desk. Go and look at the leaflets that the other students made. Can you learn anything about your area?

5 Evaluation

Discuss with the people in your class:

- Did you work well in your group?
- Did you learn new things about your area?
- Would you like to develop your leaflet?
- Do you need more time on your leaflet?
- How can you do it better next time?

26 Culture matters — Britain ~~is~~ was an island

Britain and the Channel Tunnel
WB Unit 26:
Help yourself with a dictionary

1 Britain was an island

Discussion

A long time ago, Britain was joined to France. Then, about 8,000 years ago, the level of the sea rose and Britain became an island. The result was the Channel.

There are many different ways to cross the Channel. You can cross:

by plane   by ferry   by hydrofoil
by catamaran   by hovercraft

Now, there is another way: by tunnel. Britain is not an island any more.

Have you been on a plane, ferry, catamaran, hydrofoil, hovercraft, or through a long tunnel? Where did you go?

2 Through the tunnel!

Listening

Today, you can travel by train direct from London to Paris. The journey is fast and comfortable. You can also take your car with you on one of the super-fast trains, made especially for the tunnel.

Listen to the train announcement. Can you answer these questions?

How long does the trip from London to Paris take?
How fast does the train go?
How long is the train in the tunnel?
How far under the sea is the tunnel?

3 One of the Wonders of the World

Reading

Look at the information about the Channel Tunnel. Find answers to these questions.

a How many train tunnels are there?
b Is the tunnel *in* the sea or *under* the sea?
c How long did it take to build it?
d Where are the drills now?

HOW DID THEY DO IT?

Three tunnels, not one

We talk about 'the Channel Tunnel' but, in fact, there are three tunnels, not one. There are two tunnels for trains and one service tunnel.

SOME FACTS ABOUT THE TUNNEL

Cost: £10,000,000,000 ($15,000,000,000)
Size: 50 km long (total)
130 m under the sea
Maximum speed of trains in the tunnel:
130 km per hour for car trains
160 km per hour for passenger trains
Journey time in the tunnel: 21 minutes
Passengers in each train: 800

MAKING THE TUNNEL

The Channel Tunnel is one of the most incredible pieces of engineering. It opened in 1994 after six years of work. To build the tunnels, they used giant drills from both France and England. These special drills moved slowly underground and put up the walls of the tunnels and put down the train tracks at the same time. The French engineers took their drill out when the work was finished. The English engineers left their drill inside the tunnel. It was too expensive to take it out.

4 A good thing or a bad thing?

Reading

Not everyone in Britain is happy about the Channel Tunnel. Read what some people say about the tunnel. Do they think it is a good [G] or a bad [B] thing?

a Millions of rats will run down the tunnel and bring diseases that we don't have here.

b This tunnel is fantastic. It means that we can now get to France much quicker. It is going to be excellent for business.

c Why do we want a tunnel? The tunnel is going to change our traditional British way of life. We are not an island any more.

d The tunnel saves me lots of time and I can do my work on the train. Before, it took hours and hours by plane or boat.

e I think it's great. I hate travelling by sea. I always feel sick. Now, with the tunnel, I can travel by train.

5 Across cultures

Discussion

How can you get from your country to the next country?
What do you think? Do you think it is a good idea to make it easier to travel from one country to another?

27 Revision and evaluation

Revision of Units 23–26
Extra practice •
WB Unit 27
Test yourself

1 How well do you know it?
Self-assessment

How well do you think you know the English you learnt in Units 23–26? Put a tick (√) in the table.

	very well	OK	a little
Ask someone to do something			
Offer someone something			
Use 'enough'			
New words			
Ask the way			

Now choose some sections to revise and practise.

2 Ask someone to do something
'could'

What can you say if …

1 The room is very cold.
2 You are very thirsty.
3 You didn't bring your pencils and pens to class.
4 You want to listen to someone's cassette.
5 You didn't understand what the teacher said.

Write your answers.

3 Offering someone something
'would'

Look at the pictures. What are the people saying? Write a sentence for each bubble (1–8).

120 Theme E

4 That's enough!

'enough'

What are the people saying? Write a sentence using 'enough' for each picture.

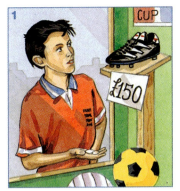   

I haven't got enough money.

5 In the factory, on the land or in the mine?

Vocabulary

Read the list of words.

aluminium   bauxite   bread   car tyres
chocolate   cocoa   copper   cotton
leather   rubber   shoes   sugar   sweets
trousers   wheat   wire

Put the names of manufactured products next to the factory.
Put the names of primary goods next to the land or the mine.

Join each primary product to the correct manufactured product.

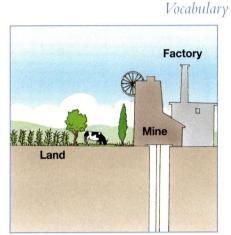

6 Asking the way

Look at the map. Write the question or the answer.

1 Excuse me, where is the bank?

   It's in Station Road, opposite the newsagent's.

2 ....

   It's in Smith Street, next to the library.

3 Could you tell me where the chemist's is, please?

   ....

4 ....

   It's in The Avenue, opposite the post office.

5 ....

   It's in School Lane, next to the school.

Unit 27 Revision and evaluation 121

7 Looking back at Units 23–26

Evaluation

7.1 Group discussion

Form groups of three or four students.
Decide, with your class, which groups will look at:

Unit 23 *or* Unit 24 *or* Units 25 and 26.

In your group, decide who will report back to the class.
Look through the Units you chose and talk about these questions:

Unit 23	Unit 24	Units 25 and 26
Did you think the topics were interesting? Did you have enough time to do the exercises?	Were the grammar exercises clear? Do you need to practise some more again?	Did you enjoy the activity? What did you learn about your area?

7.2 Future lessons

Write down any suggestions you have for future lessons.
Give your paper to your teacher at the end of the lesson.

8 Learning to use the dictionary

Help yourself

Work by yourself. Answer the questions with a tick (√).

	always	often	sometimes	never
1 Do you use a bilingual dictionary?	☐	☐	☐	☐
2 Do you use a dictionary to help you with your spelling?	☐	☐	☐	☐
3 Do you use a dictionary to help you with pronunciation?	☐	☐	☐	☐
4 Do you use a dictionary to help you find the meaning of new words?	☐	☐	☐	☐
5 Do you have a dictionary with you in class, or near you when you are working at home?	☐	☐	☐	☐

Compare your answers with your neighbour and other people in your class. Look at the Workbook Unit 25 for ideas about using a dictionary.

Open plan

Do it yourself!

See Unit 24 Exercise 6.

Make notes about what you plan to do.

Do it yourself! PLAN

Bring to class:

Do in class:

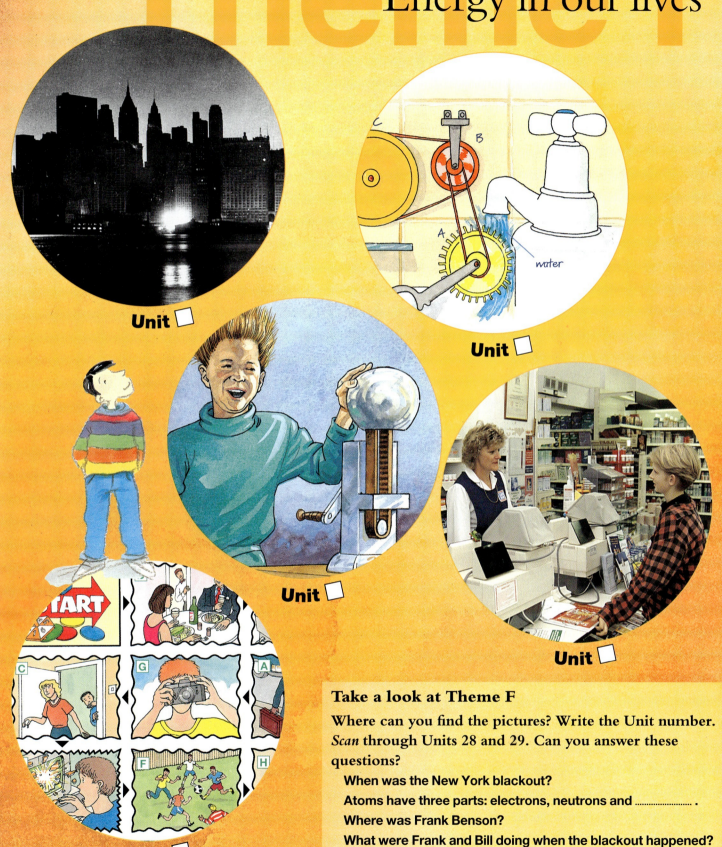

Topic 28 Blackout!

The New York blackout; electricity; curriculum link with Physics

1 Electricity in your town

Discussion

Work with a partner. You have three minutes. Make a list of the ways that you use electricity in your town. Think about:

in the streets   in shops and offices   in factories   in schools   in your home

After three minutes, compare your list with other students.

2 When the lights went out …

Brainstorming; reading

2.1 What happened?

Extra practice •
WB Ex. 2, 3

In November 1965, 30 million people in the United States and Canada lost electricity for a complete day. What do you think happened as a result? Brainstorm your ideas with the rest of the class.

> The street lights didn't work.

> The schools closed.

2.2 The Great American blackout

Now read this newspaper article about the blackout. How many things on your list from Exercise 2.1 are in the article? What other things happened?

[+] = underground in the UK
[++] = lifts in the UK
[+++] = flats in the UK

🎧 You can listen to the news story on the cassette.

Wednesday, 10 November 1965

BLACKOUT IN NEW YORK

250,000 people trapped in the subway[+]

There was panic in New York last night. Lights, elevators[++], and trains all stopped working in the biggest blackout in American history. Over 30 million people had no electricity over an area of 200,000 km^2, including New York, Boston and other large cities in the United States and Canada. Engineers are working at this moment to repair the generators.

The blackout happened at 5.30pm when many people were going home. More than 250,000 people were using the New York subway. Many people were trapped when they discovered that they could not open the train doors. In apartments[+++] and offices, people were trapped in the elevators.

There was also trouble at a prison near Boston last night, where prisoners were fighting. Thousands of police had to go to control them. At the same time, in other big towns, people broke the windows of shops and took things.

In New York last night, the only lights were from the cars. The traffic signals were not working so the cars could not move. Thousands of people could not get home so they slept in the streets in New York. Planes could not land at New York airport.

The trouble began when the hydro-electric generator at Niagara broke down. The generator

2.3 What did the police say?

What do you think the police said to the people on the streets in New York? Tell the class your ideas.

Now listen. What *did* the police say?

> Don't panic. Stay calm ...

What do you think the police said to people who were:
– in the subway?
– in the prison, near Boston?
– taking things from the shops?

Say it clearly!
/dəʊnt/ Don't

3 Decide ...

Choose an exercise. You can work by yourself, with a partner or in a small group.

Exercise 3.1 checks your vocabulary.
Exercise 3.2 checks your understanding.
Exercise 3.3 gives you more speaking practice.

3.1 Check your vocabulary *Vocabulary*

Read the news story. Make a list of words or phrases that you don't understand.

<u>Words/phrases I don't understand</u>   <u>Meaning/translation</u>

Read the story again carefully. Can you guess any meanings? Add them to your list. Check other words in your dictionary. Then check your list with your teacher.

3.2 Check how much you understand *Reading comprehension*

Is the information in these sentences true (✓), false (✗), or not in the story (?)

1 They don't know why the blackout happened. ☐
2 Some people died in the blackout. ☐
3 The blackout happened on a Sunday. ☐
4 The traffic lights were the only lights that were working. ☐
5 The blackout lasted three days. ☐
6 The police went to stop trouble at a prison. ☐
7 The blackout also happened in San Francisco. ☐
8 The airport was closed. ☐

For each false sentence, write a true one. Check your answers with your teacher.

3.3 Make an interview *Speaking*

Work with a partner. Imagine that you can interview someone who was in the blackout. You can interview:

someone who was in an elevator   someone who was in his/her car
someone who was on a subway train   a policeman

What questions can you ask? Brainstorm your ideas.

Now prepare an interview between someone who was in the blackout and a newspaper reporter. Act out your interview for other students, or for the class.

Where were you going?   When ...?   What did you do?   How ...?   How many ...?   Why ...?   What ...?   How long ...?

4 Where does electricity come from? *Reading*

The blackout happened because of a problem at the generator.
But how does electricity come to your house? Look at the diagram.
Match the sentences (a–d) to the spaces (1–4).

a This reduces the number of volts to 110 or 220.
b The hot water becomes steam.
c This makes a lot of heat.
d The electricity goes to a transformer.

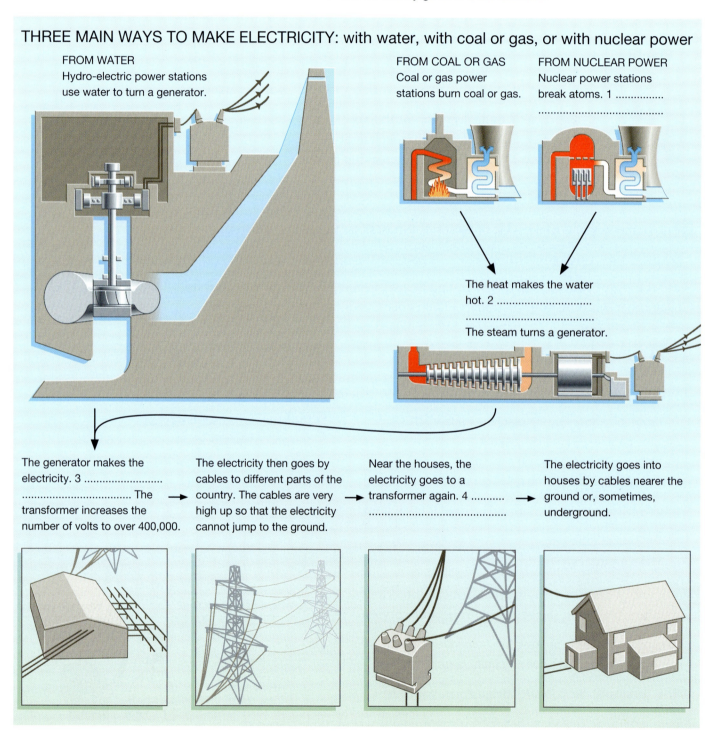

How do they make electricity in your country?
Is there a power station near you? How does electricity come to your house?
If you don't know the answers, see if you can find out for next lesson.

5 The mysteries of electricity

Discussion; reading
Extra practice • WB Ex. 1

5.1 What do you know?

Why do these things happen?
Tell the class your ideas.

5.2 Are you right?

Read part of a book on electricity and see if you are right.

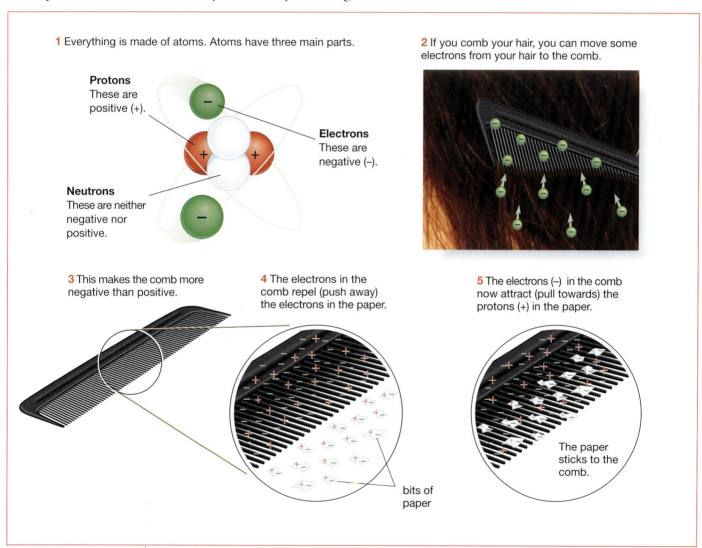

1 Everything is made of atoms. Atoms have three main parts.

Protons These are positive (+).

Electrons These are negative (–).

Neutrons These are neither negative nor positive.

2 If you comb your hair, you can move some electrons from your hair to the comb.

3 This makes the comb more negative than positive.

4 The electrons in the comb repel (push away) the electrons in the paper.

5 The electrons (–) in the comb now attract (pull towards) the protons (+) in the paper.

The paper sticks to the comb.

bits of paper

Look at the pictures in Exercise 5.1 again. Can you explain what is happening?

6 Sing a song! I didn't do it

Listen to 'I didn't do it (but all the lights went out)' and sing it with your class. The words are on page 156.

7 Decide …

Choose an exercise. You can work by yourself, with a partner or in a group.

Exercise 7.1 practises writing about a picture.
Exercise 7.2 practises using your imagination to write.
Exercise 7.3 … Do it yourself!

7.1 Dangers in the home   *Guided writing*

Look at the picture.
What dangers are there?
Write a list. For example:

There are too many plugs in the adaptor.

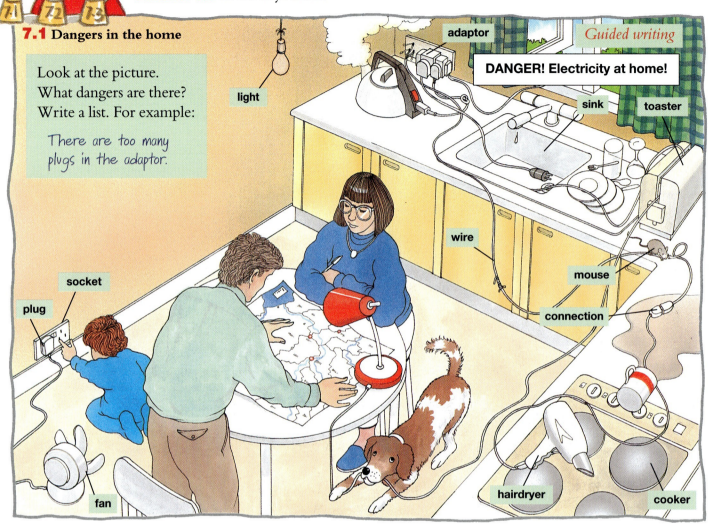

7.2 What happened next?   *Free writing*

Look at the picture. What happened next? What did the man do?
What did the woman do? What did the baby do? Write a short paragraph.

Suddenly, …

7.3 Do it yourself!   *DIY*

Decide what you want to do and then ask your teacher.
You can use the *Ideas list* on pages 150–1 to make an exercise for your class *Exercise Box*.

8 Your Language Record

Now complete your *Language Record*.

Language Record

Write the meaning of the words in your language. Add some examples.

Word	Meaning	Example
a cable		Electricity comes to our houses in cables.
a generator		A generator produces electricity.
a signal		The traffic signals were not working.
a transformer		A transformer changes the number of volts.
calm		Stay calm!
main		There are three main ways to make electricity.
panic		There was panic in New York.
trouble		What's the trouble?
be trapped		People were trapped in the lifts.
break down		My car has broken down.
burn		
control		The police had to control the prisoners.
happen		
land		The planes could not land.
turn		

Choose five more words. Write their meanings and examples.

> repel   jump   attract   a plug   a hairdryer   a prison   the ground   a comb   stick (verb)

Time to spare? Choose one of these exercises.

1. Write an exercise for your class *Exercise Box* (use the *Ideas list* on pages 150–1) or choose one to do. Check your answers on the back of the paper.
2. Look around your classroom. How many things use electricity? (Remember: batteries produce electricity.) Make a list.
3. Imagine *you* were in New York when the blackout happened. What were you doing? What did you do when the lights went out? Write a few sentences:

   When the blackout happened, I was …   I …

Language focus

Past continuous; imperatives; asking the way (2)

1 In the blackout

Listening

Frank Benson was in New York during the blackout. Listen to what happened to him.

'It was terrible. I was in the elevator+. I was going home. It was about half past five, I think. I was talking to my friend, Bill, when suddenly the elevator stopped. The lights went out. We couldn't see anything. Nothing. It was very frightening. We didn't know what had happened. People started screaming in other parts of the building.'

+ = lift in the UK

What do you think Frank and Bill did in the elevator?
Compare your ideas with others in your class.
Now listen to the next part and find out.
How do you think they came out? Listen to the last part and find out.

2 Check how much you understood

Listening

How many of these questions can you answer?

1 Where was Frank going?
2 What time did the elevator stop?
3 What was he doing when the elevator stopped?
4 What were Frank and Bill doing when they heard the voice?
5 What were the policemen and women doing?
6 How long did it take to come down?
7 What was happening outside in the street?

Listen again to complete or check your answers. Compare your answers with other students in your class. A copy of the tapescript is on page 142.

3 A new verb form

Past continuous

Extra practice •
WB Exs. 1–3
Extra practice •
TB Ws. 29.1

3.1 The verb forms you know

So far you have seen four main verb forms:

The PRESENT SIMPLE for descriptions or habits: I go to school by bus.
The PRESENT CONTINUOUS for actions that are happening now: Hurry up! What are you doing?
The PAST SIMPLE for actions that are finished: Dinosaurs lived millions of years ago.
'GOING TO' to talk about the future: What are you going to do tomorrow?

Theme F

Another useful verb form is the PAST CONTINUOUS: I was going home when the elevator stopped.

Look at the tapescript on page 142.
How many examples of the Past continuous can you find? Write some down.

I was going home.

How do you say those sentences in your language?

How can you describe the Past continuous? Complete the chart.

I, You, He, She, It We, You, They	+	+

3.2 What's it for?

What do you think you *use* the Past continuous for?
Here are some more examples from the news story in Unit 28.

The blackout happened when many people **were going** home.
More than 250,000 people **were using** the subway when the blackout happened.

Discuss it with your neighbour for a few minutes and then tell the class your ideas.

3.3 In the background

You can use the Past continuous to describe the background for another action.

More than 250,000 people WERE USING the subway ...

... when the blackout happened.

Frank and Bill WERE SINGING ...

... when they heard a voice.

3.4 MORE PRACTICE

Work in pairs. Ask your partner these questions.

– What were you doing when the teacher came into the room?
– What were you doing at eight o'clock last night?
– What were you doing last Sunday morning?
– What were you wearing at this time last week?

Invent some more questions of your own!

Write your answers to some of the questions.

(What were you ... when ...?)

When the teacher came into the room, I was ...
At six o'clock this morning, I was ...

3.5 Play a game!

In a small group of two to four students, play a game to practise the Past continuous.

HOW TO PLAY
You will need:
- some coins or counters
- a dice or spinner

1 Put your counters on START.
2 Throw the dice and move your counter.
3 If you land on a picture, write down what **was happening** or what **happened** For example:

She was walking into the room ...

... when the water came down.

4 The winner is the first person to find both halves of four sentences.

4 Do this! Don't do that!

Imperatives
Extra practice • WB Ex. 3

4.1 Don't panic!

In Unit 28, you heard some examples of instructions, like this:

Don't panic!   Don't go into the subway!   Don't run.   Stay calm!   Put your lights on!   Walk slowly.

In grammar, this is the *imperative*. In English, it's easy to tell people what to do:

  Infinitive: Stay calm!   Wait here.

It's also easy to tell people what they can't do:

  Don't + infinitive: Don't run!   Don't wait for me.

To sound more friendly, say 'please'!

Please wait here.   Please don't wait for me.

How do you give orders in your language?

4.2 Keep fit!

Your teacher or a student will give you instructions.
Be careful to follow them exactly!

> Touch your head!
>
> Clap your hands!
>
> Don't clap your hands!

4.3 MORE PRACTICE

Here's a machine you know! How do you use it?
First, label the parts.

- a cassette
- the cassette door
- headphones
- the play button
- the rewind button
- the stop/eject button

Now write some instructions on how to use it.

1 Put the headphones on your head.
2 Open ...

Add some things that you mustn't do.

Important!
Don't touch the tape.
Don't ...

5 Out and about with English

Asking the way (2)
Extra practice • WB Ex. 4
Extra practice •
TB Ws. 29.2

5.1 Left or right?

Can you match the phrase to the correct picture?

a Turn left.
b Turn right.
c Go straight on.
d Take the second turning on the left.
e Take the third turning on the right.
f It's on the corner.
g Turn left at the traffic lights.

5.2 Helen, Will and the concert hall

Helen and Will are still looking for the concert hall.
Listen to their conversations. Look at the map on page 113.
What street is the tourist information office in?

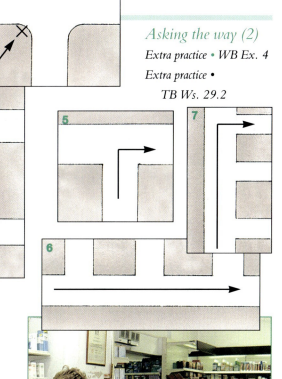

HELEN: We're not going to find the concert hall. Let's forget it.
WILL: Come on, Helen! I told you. We have to ask someone. I can ask in the chemist's.
WOMAN: Yes, dear?
WILL: Could you tell me where the concert hall is?
WOMAN: The concert hall? There isn't a concert hall in this town.
WILL: Oh, no! We saw a poster for a concert tomorrow.

WOMAN:	Oh, I see. The concert hall is in Bington, the next town, but you can buy tickets here in the tourist information office.
WILL:	Oh, good! That's what we were looking for.
WOMAN:	OK, well it's not far, but it's a bit complicated. You go out here and turn left. Then you turn left again at the traffic lights. Go straight on, and take the second turning on the left. The tourist information office is on the right, on the corner.
WILL:	Oh, dear! I go left and left again. Then it's the second turning on the left and the office is on the right. On a corner.
WOMAN:	That's right.
WILL:	Oh, thank you. I think I can remember. Bye.
WOMAN:	Bye.
HELEN:	Well, did you find out?
WILL:	The concert hall is in the next town! But we can buy tickets in the tourist information office, here.
HELEN:	Where's that?
WILL:	Well, we go left and then left again … or is it right? No, it's left, and then left, and then right. Or is it straight on? Oh, no! I can't remember!

5.3 Now you try it

Look at the map on page 113. You are at the bus station. Choose two places and write directions to get there. Don't say which place it is! Read your directions to your neighbour. He/she has to guess which place it is.

6 Do it yourself!

DIY

Look back at Units 28 and 29. What practice do *you* need? What would *you* like to do?

write an exercise	sing a song	play a game	write a letter	make a puzzle
make a dialogue	discuss something	make a test	read something	… *you decide!*

Decide by yourself or with other students what you will do in the *Do it yourself!* plan on page 141. Make some notes in the space there.

7 Your Language Record

Now complete your *Language Record*.

Time to spare? Choose one of these exercises.

1 Write an exercise for your class *Exercise Box* (use the *Ideas list* on pages 150–1) or choose one to do. Check your answers on the back of the paper.
2 Look at Exercise 4.3 again. Write instructions on how to record your voice on a cassette player.
3 Look at Exercise 5.1 again. Write directions on how to get from:
a) your house to school, and b) from your house to a friend's house.

Language Record

Your own phrase book! **ASKING THE WAY (2)**

Add more phrases. Write the meaning in your language.

> Turn left. ....
> Turn right. ....
> Go straight on. ....
> Take the second turning on the left. ....
> Take the third turning on the right. ....
> It's on the corner. ....
> Turn left at the traffic lights. ....
> ....

Past continuous = 'was/were' + verb + '-ing'
Write some examples.
Last night, at eight o'clock, I was …

My friend, …, was …
My friends, … and …, were …

Imperative = ('don't' +) infinitive
Write some more examples.
Don't panic!   Stay calm!   Stand up!   Sit down!

Revision box Adverbs

1 Adverbs. Do you remember what an adverb is? Complete the sentence.

Adjectives tell us how something is.
   She's a careful worker.   He's a dangerous driver.

Adverbs tell us ....
   She works carefully.   He drives dangerously.

2 Most adverbs have '-ly' at the end, some have '-ily', and some are different. Write the adverb.

careful → carefully
slow → ....
happy → ....
good → well

dangerous → dangerously
quick → ....
easy → ....
fast → ....

Choose an adverb for each sentence.
1 Can you speak more .... , please?
2 He plays football very ....
3 You can .... do this exercise.
4 How .... can you run?
5 If there is a fire, don't run! Walk ....

3 Play the adverb game. Mime an action. The others have to guess what you are doing.

> You're driving dangerously!
> You're opening a box carefully!
> You're running fast!

Activity 30 Save your energy!

A new invention
Extra practice •
WB Unit 30

In this Unit, you can invent a new way of saving your energy!
You will need some paper and some coloured crayons.

Before your lesson: getting ideas

1 A strange invention

Look at this invention. It helps to save your energy.
With your neighbour, see if you can explain what happens.

If you pull the handle, the train moves towards the bricks. The bricks ...

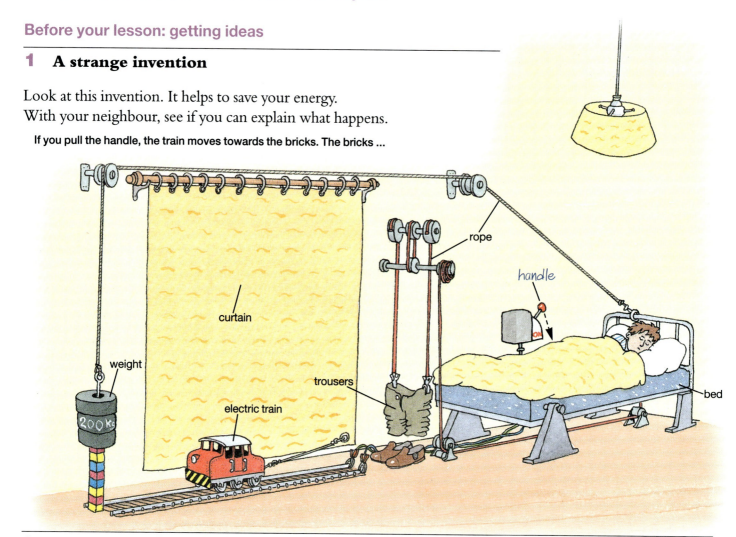

2 Your own inventions

What other things can you invent to save *your* energy at home?
Brainstorm your ideas with the class.

- A way to put your clothes on.
- A way to take the dog for a walk without leaving home.
- A way to make your bed.
- A way to wash your face.
- A way to clean your teeth.

Save energy at home

How could you save energy? Tell the class your ideas.

3 At home, invent something

Choose a topic and, at home, invent something.
Draw a picture to show how it works. Label the parts.

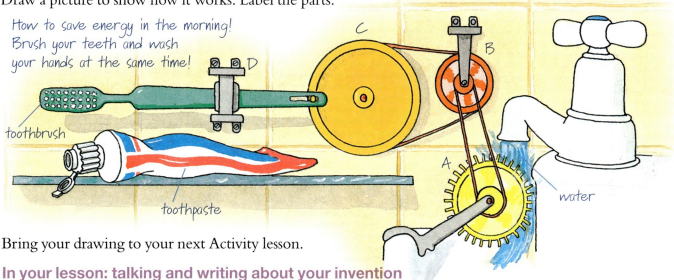

*How to save energy in the morning!
Brush your teeth and wash your hands at the same time!*

toothbrush
toothpaste
water

Bring your drawing to your next Activity lesson.

In your lesson: talking and writing about your invention

4 Explain your invention

Sit in a small group.
Show your invention to other students.
Explain how it works.

> You put some toothpaste on the brush.
> Then you turn on the water. The water …

Now write about your invention. Write some instructions and an explanation.

*Put some toothpaste on the brush. Turn on the water and wash your hands.
The water turns Wheel A. Wheel A turns Wheel B. Wheel B turns Wheel C.
When Wheel C turns, the toothbrush moves backwards and forwards.
Put your mouth in front of the toothbrush and it cleans your teeth!*

Help each other with words, spellings, and grammar.
Look in your books and ask your teacher for help, too.

5 Look at the other inventions

Put your invention on the wall or on your desk.
Go and look at the other inventions.
Ask the person who made it to tell you about it.
Which invention do you think is the best?

6 Evaluation

Discuss these questions with your class.

- Was it difficult to think of an invention?
- Was it difficult to write about it?
- Would you like to spend more time on your invention?
- Would you like to invent another thing?
- How can you do it better next time?

Unit 30   Activity   137

31 Culture matters — Energy at home

Homes in Britain and your country; reading, discussing and writing
WB Unit 31: Help yourself with fluency

1 Energy in your home

Discussion

Do most people in your country live in houses or flats?
Do you have to heat your home, or cool it? How do you do it?
What are normal temperatures in your town in the warmest and coldest months?

2 Brrrrr!

Reading and discussion

Read about energy in homes in Britain.
Do homes in Britain use more or less energy than homes in your country? Why?

In Britain, the climate is not very good. There are very few hot days and it rains a lot. Because of this, people spend a lot of time at home. Generally, British homes have a lot of furniture in them, carpet on the floors and heavy curtains.

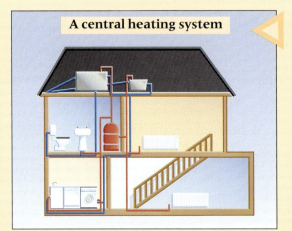

A central heating system

Because of the climate, people in Britain have to spend a lot of money on heating. Many houses have a special system called 'central heating'. This heats all the rooms and, at the same time, heats the hot water. Houses without central heating often have gas, electric or coal fires. The rooms in most British houses are quite small.

Average temperatures in December and June

Edinburgh 3.3°C/14°C
Liverpool 4.5°C/15°C
Cardiff 4.4°C/15.6°C
Plymouth 5.6°C/17.2°C
London 5.1°C/16.5°C

Many houses in Britain are cold! Many of them are over 100 years old. Often, they do not have enough insulation and the heat goes out through the walls, the windows, the doors and up the chimney.

How heat gets out

20% through the roof
10% through the windows
25% through the walls
25% up the chimney
10% through the doors
10% under doors and around windows

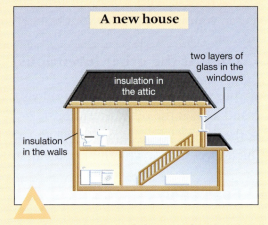

A new house

two layers of glass in the windows
insulation in the attic
insulation in the walls

New houses are much better. They have two, or sometimes three, layers of glass in the windows to stop the heat going out. In the attic, and between the walls, they have thick insulation.

How are old houses and new houses different in your country?

3 An energy plan

Drawing and writing

Look at this plan of a 'typical' modern house in England. Can you label the rooms and some of the things in them?

bathroom   kitchen   lounge/dining room   bedroom   hall
a radio   a television   a video   a cooker   a lamp   a computer
a heater   a hi-fi   a washing machine

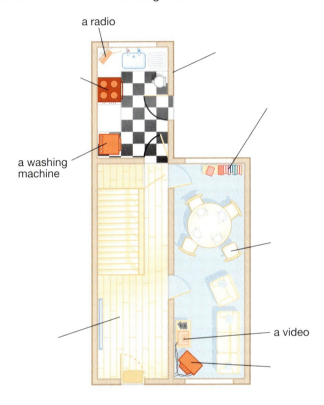
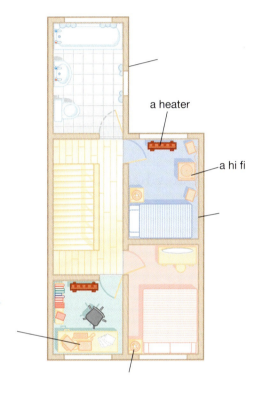

The plan shows how much energy things use.

- ■ = a lot (over 500 Watts electricity)
- ■ = a medium amount (100-500 Watts electricity)
- □ = not very much (under 100 Watts electricity)

Draw a plan of your house. Label the rooms and the things in them. At home, find out how much energy they use (ask an adult to help you) and then colour each thing.

4 Across cultures

Writing

Imagine that you are telling some people from another country about houses and homes in your country. What can you tell them? Work with your neighbour and make a list of points.

Look back at Exercises 1–3 for ideas.

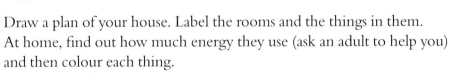

Most people live in …   Because of this, …   People spend …
The climate is …   People have to …   The houses have …
                                       The rooms are …

Read out your ideas to the rest of the class. Do they agree with you?

Unit 31   Culture matters   139

32 Revision and evaluation

Revision of Units 28–31;
design your own test

*Extra practice • WB
Unit 32*

In this Unit, you can design your own test for your class.
You can decide WHAT to test and HOW to test it.

1 What did you learn?

Things you learned

Work in a group. Look through Units 28-31. What did you learn? Make some lists.

<u>Topics</u> <u>Grammar points</u> <u>Examples of vocabulary</u> <u>'Out and about'</u>
electricity Past continuous blackout, generator

Compare your list with the other groups. Do you need to add anything to your list?

2 Who can do what?

Plan a test

With your class, decide *what* each group can write a test about.
In your group, decide *how* you can test it. You can look at Units 7, 12, 17, 22 and 27
for ideas and the *Ideas list* on pages 150–1. Here are some more ideas.

Describe a situation
You want to go from here to the bus station.
What do you say?

Draw a picture
Write some questions about it.

Write a short text
Write some questions *or* mix up the
sentences *or* take out some words.

Find a short text
Write some questions *or* mix up the
sentences *or* take out some words.

Record some questions on a cassette
Leave space for people to say their answers.

Write some 'Tell me …' sentences:
Tell me where you live.   Tell me about your family.
Tell me what you did yesterday.

3 Talk about your plan

Discussion

Tell the class what you plan to do.
Agree with your teacher what you are going to put in your part of the test.

4 Write your part of the test

Write a test

Ask your teacher for help, if you need it. Write the answers on a separate piece of
paper. When you are ready, give your part of the test to your teacher to correct.
Put it together, and do the test!

5 A test about Units 3–32 …

Look at this Unit again. You can also design a test about the whole book!

6 Write a letter to us!

You are nearly at the end of the book. Write a letter to us and tell us what you enjoyed in the book, what you found easy or difficult. Do you have any suggestions for new books?

Before you write your letter, discuss your ideas with your class. You can talk about:

Topic Units	Language focus Units
the Activities	Culture matters Units
the Exercise Box	the Ideas list
the Language Records	the songs
the games	the Workbook

Send your letter to:

or send a fax to:

++ 44 1223 325984

or send an e-mail message to:

aldh@cup.cam.ac.uk

Many thanks!

A letter to the authors

Dear Andrew and Diana,

We are in Class......... in............
in ....We are using............ School
We liked...........
The best parts of the book were..........
The parts we didn't like so much were..........
We would like to have............

Andrew Littlejohn and Diana Hicks
c/o Cambridge University Press
The Edinburgh Building
Shaftesbury Road
Cambridge
CB2 2RU
England

7 Learning to be fluent

Work by yourself. Answer the questions with a tick (√).

	always	often	sometimes	never
1 Do you speak English in class?	☐	☐	☐	☐
2 Do you have to think before you speak?	☐	☐	☐	☐
3 Do you feel silly when you speak?	☐	☐	☐	☐
4 Can you say what you want to say?	☐	☐	☐	☐
5 Do you think about grammar before you speak?	☐	☐	☐	☐

Compare your answers with others in your class. Look at Workbook Unit 31 for ideas about fluency.

Open plan

Do it yourself!

See Unit 29 Exercise 6.

Make notes about what you plan to do.

Do it yourself!
PLAN

Bring to class:

Do in class:

Answers to Unit 12, Revision and evaluation: Exercise 2

A The plant was on the table but now it's on the floor. The books were on the table but now they're on the floor. The dog was near the door but now it's under the table. The cats were under the table but now they're on the table.
B Peter cleaned the car. Helen washed her hair. Peter walked to town. Helen watched television. **C** c–d–a–b. **D a** dinosaurs; **b** trees; **c** clouds; **d** dark; **e** birds; **f** reptiles.

Answers to Unit 22, Revision and evaluation: Exercise 2

A 1 desert; **2** burn; **3** above; **4** destroy; **5** level; **6** heavily; **7** kind; **8** warm; **9** flat; **10** have.
B 1 F; **2** T; **3** F; **4** F; **5** F; **6** F; **7** ?; **8** T. **C 1** I'm going to see a film. **2** They're going to play football. **3** We're going to buy … . **4** She's going to have a party. **5** He's going to start … .
D On Monday at 4 pm Simon has to go to the dentist. On Tuesday at 7 pm he has to go to a guitar lesson. On Wednesday afternoon at 1.30 he has to go to basketball practice. On Thursday evening at 6 pm he has to go to Anne's party. On Friday he has to tidy his bedroom. On Saturday he has to buy a present for his grandmother. On Sunday afternoon at 3 pm he has to go swimming with his Uncle Jack.

Tapescript for Unit 29, Language focus: The New York blackout

PART A: 'It was terrible. I was in the elevator. I was going home. It was about half past five, I think. I was talking to my friend, Bill, when suddenly the elevator stopped. The lights went out. We couldn't see anything. Nothing. It was very frightening. We didn't know what had happened. People started screaming in other parts of the building.'

PART B: 'We shouted "Help! Help!" for hours, but nobody came. Inside the elevator, it became very hot. There was very little air in there and it was difficult to breathe. We tried to open the doors but it was impossible. Then we sat down and waited. After a while, Bill had an idea. I lifted him up and he opened the lid in the ceiling. We were very worried, but at least we had fresh air. We started to sing. Lots of old songs from when we were children!'

PART C: 'We waited over an hour, I think. Outside, people were running and shouting on the stairs. We were singing a song when suddenly we heard a voice and saw a light. Someone was shouting down to us. "Climb out of the elevator! The doors are open up here." In a few minutes, we were on top of the elevator. There was a ladder on the wall. We climbed up the ladder and then out through the doors. There were some policemen and women there. They were helping everybody. When we were all out of the elevator, they took us down the stairs. Forty-five floors, with almost no light. It took about an hour to come down. Outside, there were thousands of people on the street. Cars weren't moving at all. There weren't any lights. Just hundreds of policemen everywhere.'

Theme trail A revision game

Questions

These are the questions for the revision game. The instructions are on page 144.

1. What can you guess from this clue? 'We know they had leather boots 4,000 years ago, so …'
2. How do aerobic exercises help you?
3. Name one country that produces cocoa beans.
4. Name three things people did not have 4,000 years ago.
5. What is the name of a machine that produces electricity?
6. What is the name of the type of climate where you live?
7. Name one 'anaerobic' sport.
8. Why are rainforests important?
9. Why do they have houses on legs in South India?
10. What type of climate do they have in Greenland?
11. What did they find with the Iceman?
12. Which is better for you: swimming or football? Why?
13. Why was there a blackout in New York?
14. How do hydro-electric stations make electricity?
15. When was the first plane flight? 1600, 1880, 1903 or 1950?
16. Where are the rainforests?
17. What do you think are four of the most important inventions in history?
18. Name two primary products in a chocolate cake.
19. What are 'exports'? What are 'imports'?
20. How can running help you?
21. Name one country that produces sugar.
22. Name three different types of climate.
23. 'Dinosaurs lived at the same time as people.' True or false?
24. What type of climate is this? 'It rains all year and it is usually very warm.'
25. How long did New York have a blackout?
26. Where are the Wollemi Pines?
27. Why are electricity cables very high up?
28. What does Susan Spencer want to do?
29. What are the oldest living things on Earth?
30. Name two types of disasters from the climate.

Answers

1 … they probably had cows. 2 You breathe more oxygen and your heart works hard. 3 Countries in Latin America (e.g. Mexico, Brazil, Peru, Argentina); Countries in Africa (e.g. Kenya, Tanzania, Guinea); Countries in Asia (e.g. India, Pakistan). 4 Televisions, cars, computers, schools, planes … and much more! 5 A generator. 6 See map on pages 152–3. 7 Football. 8 They help to make oxygen, they give us many medicines, and thousands of types of animals live there. 9 Because it rains a lot and they often have floods. 10 A polar climate. 11 Arrows, a bow, boots and an axe. 12 Swimming – it is an aerobic sport. 13 There was a problem with the generator. 14 Water turns the generator. The generator makes electricity. 15 1903. 16 In South America, Asia, Australia and Africa. 17 See page 64 for some ideas. 18 Sugar, cocoa, wheat, milk. 19 Exports are things that a country sells to another country. Imports are things that a country buys from another country. 20 It makes your heart work hard. 21 Brazil, Cuba, India. 22 Polar, tropical, mountain, cool temperate, warm temperate, tundra, desert, monsoon. 23 False. 24 Tropical. 25 One day. 26 Australia. 27 So that the electricity cannot jump to the ground. 28 She wants to swim for England in the Olympic games and win a gold medal. 29 Trees. 30 Hurricanes, floods, no water.

Unit 13
Qs: 1, 4, 11, 15, 17

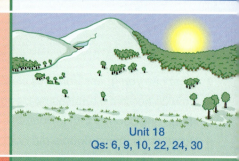

Unit 18
Qs: 6, 9, 10, 22, 24, 30

Language Box

Unit 3
Qs: 2, 7, 12, 20, 28

Instructions

What you need

a dice … … or spinner … … and some counters

Aim

To be the first person to answer correctly one question from four *Topic* Units and one question from the *Language Box*.

How to play

1. Play in a group of two to four people.
2. Copy this chart:

Unit 3 ☐	Unit 18 ☐	
Unit 8 ☐	Unit 23 ☐	
Unit 13 ☐	Unit 28 ☐	
Language Box ☐		

3. Everybody starts at START.
4. Each person throws the dice and moves forward the number it shows.
5. If you land on a *Unit* or *Language Box* square, choose a question number. (Don't look at the questions first!) Cross it off [X] the square. The questions are on page 143.
6. If you answer correctly, tick the box on your chart.
   (The others can check the answers on page 143).
7. The first person to answer one question from FOUR *Topic* Units and ONE from the *Language Box* correctly is the winner.
8. You can only ask each question once.

Unit 8
Qs: 8, 16, 23, 26, 29

START

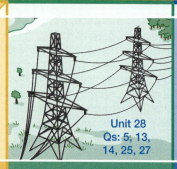

Unit 28
Qs: 5, 13, 14, 25, 27

Language Box

Unit 8
Qs: 8, 16, 23, 26, 29

Unit 23
Qs: 3, 18, 19, 21

Language Box

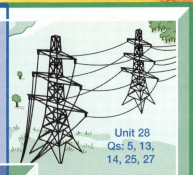
Unit 28
Qs: 5, 13, 14, 25, 27

Language Box

1. What is the Past simple of 'write'?
2. What is the regular Past tense ending?
3. What is the Past simple of 'find'?
4. Say a sentence with: 'don't mind'.
5. Complete the sentence: He's a very bad driver. He drives very … .
6. You want to know how to write a word. What do you say?
7. Say two things about your plans for next week.
8. You want someone to say something again. What do you say?
9. You want someone to open the window. What do you say?
10. Say three things you have to do tomorrow.
11. Say two things you were doing before your English lesson started.
12. Give instructions to go from your school to the nearest bank.

Unit 13
Qs: 1, 4, 11, 15, 17

Language Box

Unit 18
Qs: 6, 9, 10, 22, 24, 30

Unit 3
Qs: 2, 7, 12, 20, 28

Unit 23
Qs: 3, 18, 19, 21

Supplementary Unit A A Parcel of English

WHAT IS A PARCEL OF ENGLISH?

A Parcel of English is something you can make to describe your school and where you live. You can include photographs, postcards, maps, recipes – almost anything. You can send your parcel to another class and receive a parcel from them. Cambridge University Press can link you to another school.

Before you do this Unit

1 Pictures of you and your town

Draw a small picture of yourself (5 cm × 5 cm) or find a passport photo. Find some postcards and photographs of your area to take to your lesson.

You also need glue, scissors and small pieces of paper.

In your Parcel of English lesson

2 What is a Parcel of English?

Look at the picture of a Parcel of English. Discuss these questions with your class.

What is in the parcel?
What can you do with your parcel?
Can you display it in your school?
Can you give it to a class in your school?
Can you send it to a school in another country?

3 What's in the Parcel of English?

What can you put in your Parcel of English to describe the people and places below? With your class, make a list of your ideas. (If you want to post your Parcel of English, remember that it can't be very big or heavy!)

You and your class
photographs

Your school
timetables

Your town
postcards

4 A picture and description of me

For the first part of your Parcel of English, you can write a short description of yourself. For example:

My name is ... I am ... old.
I live ...   I have ...
In my free time, I like to ... .
My favourite subjects at school are ... .

Put your picture on a small piece of paper.
Write your description next to it.
Your teacher will put all your descriptions together.

5 What can you write?

Divide into groups of three or four students. First, with your class, decide which part of the Parcel of English (a–d) each group will write.

Your town
a Where people work.
b Where people go in their free time.

Your school
c A description of your school.
d The subjects and timetable.

Here are some examples:

About our town

Where people work in our town
Our town has changed a lot in the last forty years. When my parents were small most people worked as farmers or fishermen. Nowadays in our town, a lot of people work in car factories, offices and banks. The factories are outside the town and the offices and banks are in the centre. In the summer, a lot of people work in the hotels near the beach.

Where people go in their free time
In our town, there are many different places to go in the evenings and at weekends. Young people like going to the swimming pools and the cinema. There are also four discos in our town. Older people like going to the beach and the restaurants. A lot of people do sports: football, swimming, and bicycle riding. There is a big new sports stadium in the centre of town and there are football matches and races there every weekend.

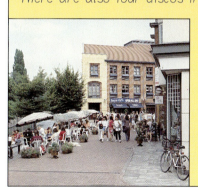

About our school

A description of our school
Our school is very new. They built it five years ago in the north of the city near the new blocks of flats. It is very big. There are 40 classrooms and 1,000 students in our school. There's a big playground and three football fields. There are 3 science laboratories and a computer room. We have two lessons a week in the computer room. On the top floor there's a big library with 5,000 books.

Our school day
We go to school five days a week. We start lessons at 8 o'clock and we go home at 3 o'clock. Most students walk to school but some students come on the bus. We have lunch from 12 o'clock to 1 o'clock. Some students eat in the canteen but most bring their own lunch. We have 8 lessons every day. One lesson is 40 minutes. The students come to our school when they are 11 years old and they stay for 6 years.

6 Making your parcel

Work in your group. First, read the examples in Exercise 5. Then, in your group, talk about and write your part of the parcel. Help each other with words and spellings. (Everybody in your group must write.)

Put your work on a piece of paper with your pictures.

Look at Exercise 3 again. In your next lesson, bring the things you thought of to school. Put them with your pictures and writing.

You now have a Parcel of English to send to another school!

Supplementary Unit B Making an Exercise Box

Writing exercises helps you learn English. In this Unit you can make a box of exercises for other students to do. You can also use the box when you have time to spare.

Writing your own exercises

1 Types of exercises

Here are two types of exercises. Can you find them in the *Ideas list* on pages 150–1? Can you do them?

2 Make an exercise

Work in a small group. Make up some exercises for other students to do.

Word halves: find 12 new words and divide each one in half. Mix up the halves and make two lists.
Write the meaning of the words in your language or draw a small picture of it.
Mixed-up sentences: find eight sentences. Mix up the words.

Write a title for the exercises (for example: Word halves) and put your name on it.
Write the answers on the back of the paper. Put the exercises in the box.

3 Take an exercise

Take an exercise from the box. See if you can do it. Don't write on the paper!
You can check your answers on the back.

4 The Ideas list

Look at the other exercises in the *Ideas list* on pages 150–1. Have you done these types of exercises before?

Choose one, and write another exercise for your class *Exercise Box*.

You can make your own exercises for homework, in the '*Decide …*' sections of this book, or when you have time to spare.

Irregular verbs

Infinitive	Past simple	Past participle
be	was, were	been
become	became	become
begin	began	begun
bite	bit	bitten
blow	blew	blown
break	broke	broken
bring	brought	brought
build	built	built
buy	bought	bought
can	could	–
catch	caught	caught
choose	chose	chosen
come	came	come
cost	cost	cost
cut	cut	cut
dig	dug	dug
do	did	done
draw	drew	drawn
drink	drank	drunk
drive	drove	driven
eat	ate	eaten
fall	fell	fallen
feed	fed	fed
feel	felt	felt
fight	fought	fought
find	found	found
fly	flew	flown
forget	forgot	forgotten
forgive	forgave	forgiven
freeze	froze	frozen
get	got	got
give	gave	given
go	went	gone
grow	grew	grown

Infinitive	Past simple	Past participle
hang	hung	hung
have	had	had
hear	heard	heard
hide	hid	hidden
hit	hit	hit
hold	held	held
hurt	hurt	hurt
keep	kept	kept
know	knew	known
lay	laid	laid
lead	led	led
lean	leant	leant
learn	learnt	learnt
	learned	learned
leave	left	left
lend	lent	lent
let	let	let
lie	lay	lain
light	lit	lit
	lighted	lighted
lose	lost	lost
make	made	made
mean	meant	meant
meet	met	met
pay	paid	paid
put	put	put
read	read	read
ride	rode	ridden
ring	rang	rung
rise	rose	risen
run	ran	run
say	said	said
see	saw	seen

Infinitive	Past simple	Past participle
sell	sold	sold
send	sent	sent
set	set	set
shake	shook	shaken
shine	shone	shone
shoot	shot	shot
show	showed	shown
		showed
shut	shut	shut
sing	sang	sung
sink	sank	sunk
sit	sat	sat
sleep	slept	slept
slide	slid	slid
speak	spoke	spoken
spell	spelt	spelt
	spelled	spelled
spend	spent	spent
spread	spread	spread
stand	stood	stood
steal	stole	stolen
stick	stuck	stuck
swim	swam	swum
swing	swung	swung
take	took	taken
teach	taught	taught
tell	told	told
think	thought	thought
throw	threw	thrown
understand	understood	understood
wake	woke	woken
wear	wore	worn
win	won	won
wind	wound	wound
write	wrote	written

Ideas list

Here are some ideas to help you make your own exercises. (Remember to put the answers and your name on the back of your card.)

Idea 1 Word halves

Choose some words and cut them in half.

- swimming
- sport
- lungs
- strong
- health
- flexible

What are the words?

Idea 2 Put the letters in the right order

Choose some words and mix up the letters.

swimming sport lungs strong
health flexible

What are the words?

trspo lxeifleb ngrtso
unslg mimwsign hleaht

Idea 3 Put the words in the right order

Choose some sentences and mix up the words.

Swimming is an excellent way to keep fit.
It makes your body very flexible.
It can make your body very strong.

What are the sentences?

1 is keep way excellent to swimming an fit
2 makes it your very body flexible
3 make it very can body your strong

Idea 4 Match the words with the pictures or the meaning

Choose some words and draw some pictures or write the meaning in your language.

swimming
sport
lungs
strong
health
flexible

Match the words with the pictures or the meaning.

swimming
sport
lungs
strong
health
flexible

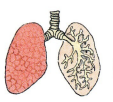 

Idea 5 Find the words

Choose some words and hide them in a square of letters. Write some clues.

Find the words.

- enjoy
- lungs
- heart
- flexible
- legs
- health
- muscles
- body
- excellent
- strong

1 To like doing something: e............
2 We breathe with our l............ .
3 h............
4 Swimming makes your body f............ .
5 l............ .
6 Sport for h............ !
7 m............ .
8 Sport can make your b............ strong and flexible.
9 Running is an e............ way to keep fit.
10 Football makes your legs s............ .

Idea 6 Put the sentences in the right order

Choose a paragraph or a dialogue. Mix up the sentences.

PETER: When did you start training?
SUSAN: Well, I started training when I was about nine. At first, I only swam an hour every day.
PETER: But now you do five hours every day.
SUSAN: That's right.
PETER: Do you enjoy training?
SUSAN: Oh, yes! I love it. I really love swimming.
PETER: What about school?
SUSAN: Well, I don't mind going to school. I hate doing homework, but school's OK.

Put the sentences in the right order.
– Do you enjoy training?
– But now you do five hours every day.
– When did you start training?
– That's right.
– What about school?
– Oh, yes! I love it. I really love swimming.
– Well, I started training when I was about nine. At first, I only swam an hour every day.
– Well, I don't mind going to school. I hate doing homework, but school's OK.

Idea 7 What's the question?

Write some questions and answers. Copy the answers. Leave space for the questions.

1 What's your name?
  My name's Steven.
2 Do you live near here?
  No, I don't. I live quite far from here.
3 Is your brother younger or older than you?
  He's older than me.

What's the question?

1 ....?
  My name's Steven.
2 ....?
  No, I don't. I live quite far from here.
3 ....?
  He's older than me.

Idea 8 Fill in the missing words

Choose a paragraph and take out some words.

Running is a good way to keep fit. Anyone can do it. Running can help to make you strong. It is very good for your legs, for your heart and your lungs. It also helps to make your body flexible. Energy level: 2.

Fill in the missing words.

Running is a .... way to keep fit. Anyone can .... it. Running can help to make .... strong. It is very good for your .... , for your heart and your lungs. It also helps to make your body .... Energy level: 2.

Idea 9 Answer the questions

Choose a paragraph and write some questions.

Running is a good way to keep fit. Anyone can do it. Running can help to make you strong. It is very good for your legs, for your heart and your lungs. It also helps to make your body flexible. Energy level: 2.

Answer the questions

1 How can running help you?
2 What is running good for?
3 How can it help your body?
4 Do you need a lot of energy?

Idea 10 True or false?

Choose a paragraph and write some true and false sentences.

Running is a good way to keep fit. Anyone can do it. Running can help to make you strong. It is very good for your legs, for your heart and your lungs. It also helps to make your body flexible. Energy level: 2.

Are these sentences true, false, or is the information not in the text?

1 Running is bad for your heart.
2 You need practice to run well.
3 Running is a very expensive sport.
4 Running makes your legs strong.

Map of the world

Polar

In polar areas, it is very cold with strong, dry winds. The temperature in the summer never rises above 10°C. The sun never rises above the horizon, even at midday.

Tropical

Places with a tropical climate are near the Equator. It is always hot there, and the temperature is usually between 24°C and 27°C. There is a lot of rain all the year. The rainforests are in these areas.

Cool temperate

In these areas they have rain almost all the year. The summers are usually warm (about 18–20°C) and winters are not very cold (usually above −3°C).

Mountain

The climate in mountain areas changes a lot with the height of the mountain. It is always colder in the mountains than in the lowlands. Sometimes, they get a lot of snow, ice and rain there.

Warm temperate
Places with a warm temperate climate have very hot, dry summers – often over 40°C. The winters there are not normally very cold.

Desert
Places with a desert climate have less than 25cm of rain each year. There are very few clouds. This means that during the day, it is very hot (up to 52°C) but at night it gets very cold.

Monsoon
In areas with a monsoon climate, there are usually two very different seasons – a wet one and a dry one. In India, for example, they have very heavy rain from June to October. Then, in October, there is a sudden change and it is very dry until about March.

Tundra
In areas with a tundra climate, there is very little rain. It is usually cold there and the summer is very short. Not many trees grow in these areas.

Map of the world

Songs

Unit 1 All around the world

There are cities, rivers, cars and mountains
All around the world.
There is ice cream, water, rice and pasta
For every boy and girl.
We can send a rocket to the moon,
Far outside this world.
There are zebras, monkeys, lions and leopards
All around the world.

Chorus
There's so much in this world
That we'll never know about,
But every boy and every girl
Can have fun finding out.

There are buses, beaches, farms and factories
All around the world.
There is music, medicine, fruit and paper
For every boy and girl.
We can use a phone to speak to friends
On the other side of this world.
There are flowers, forests, fish and dolphins
All around the world.

Repeat chorus

Unit 3 Sports for everybody

I go out cycling every day,
I get strong and fit that way,
And I play football at weekends,
With all my other healthy friends.
We like to run and swim and walk
Let's move around, no time to talk!
So we enjoy sport anyway,
We love to do sport every day.

Chorus
Yes there are sports for everybody.
You don't have to stay in and watch television.
Choose a healthy hobby.
The fun never ends when you play
  with your friends,
With your friends,
When you play with your friends.

If the weather is OK,
We can go fishing all the day.
We can jog around the park,
It's very good for the heart.
Yes, we like to swim and run and walk,
Let's move around, no time to talk!
So we enjoy sport anyway,
We love to do sport every day.

Repeat chorus

Unit 8 Mother forest

The forest is strong with a perfume so sweet
Such a perfect place to dream.
She feeds from the earth, from the water and air,
Mother nature, pure and green.

A humming bird sings high above,
Her feathers shine in the sun,
While deep in the jungle it's cool and it's dark,
And a tiger is feeding her young.

Chorus
Save our trees!
Don't cut them all down.
Save our trees!
Don't cut them all down.

They shelter the flowers
  from the sun and the wind,
Helping them bloom and grow.
They care for the creatures that hide in the leaves,
Every colour of a rainbow.

But men with machines want to cut her down,
So how can we make people see
That our forest is rich with the beauty of life?
So sing out a warning with me …
Repeat chorus

Unit 13 Pyramids and dinosaurs (a long, long, long time ago)

I was a baby, but I am sure
I can't remember when I was born,
When I only ate and I only cried,
I suppose a few years is a very long time.
But a history book changes it all,
You thought you were big, but you know that you're small
When you read about pyramids and dinosaurs.

Chorus
That was a long,
Ooh, it was a long, long,
That was a long, long, long time ago.

I was a baby, but I don't think
I can remember a single thing
About when I couldn't talk and I couldn't laugh,
I suppose it must be so far in the past.

But a history book changes it all,
You thought you were big, but you know that you're small
When you read about pyramids and dinosaurs.

Repeat chorus

Unit 18 Here comes the sun

Chorus
Here comes the sun,
Here comes the sun, and I say 'It's all right'.

Little darling, it's been a long, cold, lonely winter.
Little darling, it feels like years since it's been here.

Repeat chorus

Little darling, the smile's returning to their faces.
Little darling, it seems like years since it's been here.

Repeat chorus

Sun, sun, sun, here it comes.

Little darling, I feel that ice is
  slowly melting.
Little darling, it seems like years since it's been clear.

Repeat chorus

Unit 23 Big money

Money! You've got big money!

They will never leave you on your own.
Money! Lock your door and disconnect the phone.

Driving in a limousine or riding on a bus,
It only takes one person to begin to make a fuss,
Soon you are surrounded, they won't let you get away,
They all want a slice of it now they know you've got …

Big money! Money!

You've got big money!
Careful who you try to call a friend.
Money! It will only fool you in the end.

Walking on a beach or sitting in a car,
It only takes one person to tell others who you are,
Soon you are surrounded, they won't let you get away,
They all want a slice of it now they know you've got …

Big money! Money!
You've got big money!
I know it will only drive me crazy.
Money! You may think that I am really lazy.

My pockets are so empty, I just dream my life away.
A friend or two is all I need to brighten up my day.
I'm free to come, I'm free to go and people are so kind.
They smile at me because they know that I have got no time for …

Money! Money!

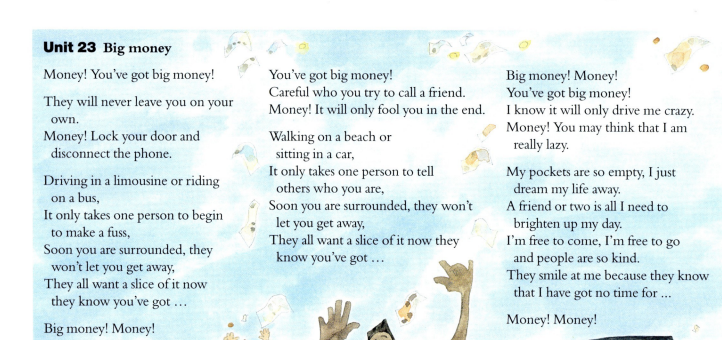

Unit 28 I didn't do it (but all the lights went out)

We were sitting at home, my friend and me,
The food was cooking, we were watching T.V.
A man was talking on the screen.
A dog was barking in my street.
I picked up the remote control,
I pushed a button and woh, oh, no, no …
I didn't do it, but all the lights went out.

I looked out of my window,
Completely dark in my road.
I couldn't see a single light,
Then my friend said 'are you all right?'
I said 'I just picked up the remote control,
I pushed a button and woh, oh, no, no …
I didn't do it, but all the lights went out.'

That was nearly a year ago.
How it happened I just don't know.
No more electricity,
No computers, no lights, and no T.V.

Here I am sitting on the floor.
Someone is knocking on my front door.
I just don't know what to do,
A policeman says 'I want to speak to you.'
I said 'I just picked up the remote control,
I pushed a button and woh, oh, no, no …
I didn't do it, but all the lights went out.'

They've got me in a police car,
They're taking me away, but it's not fair,
I didn't do it, but all the lights went out.

Wordlist/Index

In this list you can find the words which appear in the *Topic*, *Language focus* and *Culture matters* Units and their page numbers. This list is also an index of the language and the grammar in the book.

Abbreviations:
adj. adjective   *adv.* adverb   *conj.* conjunction
interj. interjection   *n.* noun   *pl.* plural
prep. preposition   *pron.* pronoun
sing. singular   *v.* verb

A

a lot of *adj.*   25
about *adv.*   11
above *adv.*   88
active *adj.*   58
activity *n.*   38
adjectives   14
adult *n.*   18
advanced *adj.*   81
adverbs   135
adverbs with '-ly', '-ily'   31
advertisement *n.*   107
aerobic *adj.*   25
affect *v.*   84
afraid *adj.*   57
Africa *n.*   17
after *prep.*   81
afternoon *n.*: in the afternoon   39
again *adv.*   27
ago *adv.*   15
air *n.*   45
Alabama *n.*   58
Alaska *n.*   58
Aldrin, Buzz *n.*   79
alive *adj.*   59
allegiance *n.*   38
almost *adv.*   50
alone *adj.*   17
already *adv.*   78
also *adv.*   25
aluminium *n.*   104
always *adv.*   39
American *adj.*   78
American football *n.*   39
anaerobic *adj.*   25
angrily *adv.*   32
angry *adj.*   32
announcement *n.*   38
another *adj.*   57
answer *v.*   30
antelope *n.*   17
any *adj.*   13
anybody *pron.*   20
anyone *pron.*   25
Appalachian Mountains *n.*   58
appear *v.*   50
archaeologist *n.*   65
Arctic *n.*   86
area *n.*   58
aren't = are not *v.*   13
Argentina *n.*   105
Arizona *n.*   59
Armstrong, Neil *n.*   79
around *adv.*   53
arrive *v.*   92
arrow *n.*   65
as … as   50
Asia *n.*   45
asking the way (1)   113
asking the way (2)   133
astronaut *n.*   79
at the same time   119
ate *v.* = *past of* 'eat'   68
atom *n.*   126
attack *v.*   81
attic *n.*   138
attract *v.*   127
Australasia *n.*   105
Australia *n.*   16
Austria *n.*   65
axe *n.*   65
Aztecs *n.*   81

B

back *n.*: at the back   50
background *n.*   131
bad *adj.*   17
badminton *n.*   24
bag *n.*   72
baker's *n.*   113
band *n.*   38
bank *n.*   16
baseball *n.*   39
basketball *n.*   39
bat *n.*   18
bathroom *n.*   139
battle *n.*   79
Battle of Little Big Horn *n.*   79
be *v.*   13
be trapped *v.*   124
beach *n.*   58
bean *n.*   81
bear *n.*   59
beat *v.*   32
beautiful *adj.*   11
because of *prep.*   16
become *v.*   25
bedroom *n.*   139
bedtime *n.*   27
before *prep.*   50
began = *past of* 'begin' *v.*   20
begin *v.*   20
behind *prep.*   114
below *prep.*   87
between *prep.*   38
big *adj.*   21
bilingual *adj.*   122
Bingham, Hiram *n.*   15
bird-watching *n.*   99
blackout *n.*   124
blood *n.*: blood circulation   25
body *n.*   25
bone *n.*   50
book *n.*   66
boot *n.*   65
border *n.*   59
boring *adj.*   16
Boston *n.*   124
both *adv.*   116
bottom *n.*: at the bottom   52
bought = *past of* 'buy' *v.*   70
bow *n.*   65
brain *n.*   79
brainstorm *v.*   36
Brazil *n.*   84
bread *n.*   37
break *n.*   38
break *v.*   124
breathe *v.*   25
bright *adj.*   14
Brilliant! *interj.*   73
brilliant *adj.*   99
bring *v.*   39
Bristlecone Pines *n.*   47
Bristol *n.*   116
Britain *n.*   138
broke = *past of* 'break' *v.*   124
broke down = *past of* 'break down' *v.*   124
bubble up *v.*   59
buffalo *n.*   59
build *v.*   99
building *n.*   13
bulb *n.*   64
burn *v.*   126
bus station *n.*   113
business *n.*   119
butter *n.*   116
butterfly *n.* (*pl.* butterflies)   14
buy *v.*   70

C

cable *n.*   126
café *n.*   93
cake *n.*   105
calculate *v.*   33
calendar *n.*   81
California *n.*   58
call *v.*   65
calm *adj.*   125
came = *past of* 'come' *v.*   70
Can I have …?   93
Canada *n.*   58
canoeing *n.*   98
canteen *n.*   38
canyon *n.*   58
capital *n.*   10
car *n.*   13
carbon dioxide *n.*   25
careful *adj.*   32
careful *adj.*: be careful   59
carefully *adv.*   33
carpet *n.*   138
catch *v.*   46
cave *n.*   16
cavepeople *n.*   11
central heating *n.*   138
certain *adj.*   92
chair *n.*   66
champion *n.*   27
Channel Tunnel *n.*   119
check *v.*   35
cheese *n.*   70
cheetah *n.*   18
chemist's *n.*   113
Chicago *n.*   58
chicken *n.*   70
children *n. pl.* (*sing.* child)   70
Chile *n.*   105
chimney *n.*   138
chimpanzee *n.*   14
China *n.*   68
chips *n.*   93
chocolate *n.*   104
choice *n.*   99
choose *v.*   11
chop *v.*   45
Civil Rights *n.*   79
civil war *n.*   78
clap *v.*   133
classroom phrases   33
clay *adj.*   81
clean *adj.*   39
climate *n.*   47
climb *v.*   21
clothes *n.*   66
cloud *n.*   46
clue *n.*   10
coal *n.*   126
coast *n.*   58
coat *n.*   77
cocoa bean *n.*   105
coin *n.*   95
cold *adj.*   15
collect *v.*   36
Collins, Ed *n.*   79
Colorado *n.*   58
comb *n.*   127
comb *v.*   127
come *v.*   16
comfortable *adj.*   99
communicate *v.*   14
company *n.*   107
comparatives and superlatives   15
compare *v.*   38
completely *adv.*   16
complicated *adj.*   134
computer *n.*   64
concert *n.*   114
concert hall *n.*   114
condition *n.*   107
conference *n.*   90
connection *n.*   128
container *n.*   110
continent *n.*   10
control *v.*   45
Coober *n.*   16
cook *v.*   67
cool *adj.*   85
copper *n.*   104
corner *n.*   133
cost *v.*   99
cotton *n.*   78
'could': *making a request*   110
country *n.*   10
countryside *n.*   99
cousin *n.*   53
cover *v.*   45
crash *v.*   50
cricket *n.*   98
crop *n.*   70
cross *v.*   118
cry *v.*   10
curtain *n.*   138

cut down v.   88
cycling n.   24

D

danger n.   45
dangerous adj.   11
dangerously adv.   31
dark adj.   45
day n.: in the day   16
dead adj.   14
deep adj.   59
delicious adj.   41
Denmark n.   65
dentist n.   16
Denver n.   58
description n.   39
desert n.   58
design v.   78
dessert n.   93
destroy v.   87
detective n.   64
Detroit n.   58
dialogue n.   34
diameter n.   33
dictionary n.   33
did = *past of* 'do' v.   11
die v.   48
different adj.   24
difficult adj.   30
dinosaur n.   11
Dinosaur National Monument n.   59
disappear v.   45
disaster n.   87
discover v.   47
discovery n. (*pl.* discoveries)   47
disease n.   119
do v.   13
doctor n.   16
doctor's n.   113
don't = do not v.   13
drag (up) v.   17
drank = *past of* 'drink' v.   71
dream n.   79
drill n.   119
drink v.   39
driver n.   32
dry adj.   16
Duluth n.   58
during prep.: during the day   59
dust n.   65
dusty adj.   16
dyke n.   87

E

Earth n.   15
easily adv.   32
east n.   58
easy adj.   14
eat v.   39
echo n.   18

'-ed' *form*   52
education n.   107
egg n.   59
Egypt n.   10
electricity n.   66
electron n.   127
electronic adj.   64
elevator n.   124
elk n.   59
empty adj.   16
encyclopaedia n.   10
energy n.   24
engineer n.   119
engineering n.   119
England n.   85
enjoy v.   30
enormous adj.   59
enough adv.   37
environment n.   90
equal adj.   79
equilateral adj.: equilateral triangle   33
equipment n.   39
especially adv.   118
Europe n.   45
European adj., n.   79
event n.   76
every adj.   22
everybody n.   16
excellent adj.   25
except adv.   39
exchange v.   14
exciting adj.   14
Excuse me …   113
exercise n.   25
expensive adj.   16
explain v.   12
explorer n.   15
export v.   105
extinct adj.   17
extra adj.   120

F

face n.   14
factory n.   107
facts n.   119
fall v.   10
false adj.   46
famous adj.   58
fan n.   50
fantastic adj.   58
farm n.   70
farmer n.   70
fast adj.   14
fast adv.   32
fasten v.   65
fat adj.   37
favourite adj.   39
feel v.   46
feel (v.) sick   119
feelings n. pl.   14
fell = *past of* 'fall' v.   87
ferry n. (*pl.* ferries)   110
few adj.   20

field n.   70
fight v.   79
filled adj.   65
find v.   15
find out v.   19
finish v.   38
finished adj.   93
fire n.   67
first adj.   79
First Aid Kit n.   88
fish n.   37
fisherman n.   81
fishing n.   24
fit adj.   25
fizzy adj.: fizzy drinks   104
flag n.   38
flat adj.   58
flexible adj.   24
flood n.   87
floor n.   138
Florida n.   87
flour n.   105
fly n.   10
fly v.   14
flying saucer n.   19
follow v.: Follow the instructions.   88
food n.   11
football n.   24
Ford, Henry n.   79
foreigner n.   107
forest fire n.   88
forever adv.   45
forget v.   133
forgot = *past of* 'forget' v.   92
fossil n.   52
fought = *past of* 'fight' v.   79
found = *past of* 'find' v.   15
France n.   10
free time n.   30
friend n.   27
friendly adj.   14
frog n.   19
front n.: at the front   50
fruit n.   37
frying pan n.   105
furniture n.   138
future n.   40

G

game n.   25
garden n.   16
gardening n.   98
gas n.   59
generally adv.   138
generator n.   124
Georgia n.   58
Germany n.   90
get v.   12
get into v.   21

get out v.   21
get up v.   27
geyser n.   59
giant adj.   119
give v.   39
global village n.   104
go v.   10
go back to v.   16
go out v.: go out with friends   30
Go straight on.   133
goat n.   70
god n.   81
going to v.   90
going to: negative and questions   91
gold n.   27
golf n.   24
good adj.   16
got = *past of* 'get' v.   12
government n.   78
grammar n.   31
Grand Canyon n.   58
grandfather n.   10
grandmother n.   10
grass n.   65
Greenland n.   84
ground n.   45
group n.   28
grow v.   11
guess v.   66
guide n.   59
Guinea n.   105
Gulf of Mexico n.   58

H

had = *past of* 'have' v.   67
had to = *past of* 'have to' v.   87
hairdryer n.   128
half n. (*pl.* halves)   87
hall n. [*AmE* = corridor; *BrE* = large room]   39
handball n.   73
happen v.   45
happily adv.   32
happy adj.   16
hard adv.   25
hard adj.   32
hate v.   24
have v.   67
have to v.   85
have to do something v.   92
Hawaii n.   58
head n.   50
head office n.   107
health n.   25
healthy adj.   11
hear v.   33
heard = *past of* 'hear' v.   130
heart n.   25
heat n.   86

heavily adv.   86
heavy adj.   50
help v.   11
hen n.   116
Here you are.   93
history n.   64
hole n.   15
home n.   72
homework n.   27
hope v.   20
horrible adj.   13
hospital n.   113
hot adj.: It is very hot   16
hovercraft n.   118
How far …?   13
How fast …?   118
How long …?   14
How much/many …?   13
How often …?   24
hundred   59
hungry adj.   14
hunt v.   17
hurricane n.   87
husband n.   16
hydro-electric adj.   126
hydrofoil n.   118

I

ice n.   68
Iceman n.   67
I'd like …   94
immediately adv.   65
imperatives   132
import v.   105
important adj.   37
impossible adj.   17
improve v.   25
in a café   93
in fact   119
in front of prep.   114
including adj.   59
increase v.   126
incredible adj.   119
incredibly adv.   87
independent adj.   78
India n.   84
Indian (adj.) languages   11
influence v.   85
information n.   59
'-ing': *special verbs with* '-ing'   30
insect n.   10
inside n.   46
instead of prep.   33
insulation n.   138
intelligent adj.   20
interesting adj.   21
interview v.   28
invent v.   74
invention n.   64
inviting and suggesting   53

iron *n.* 104
irregular Past simple 70
island *n.* 81
Italy *n.* 65

J

Java *n.* 45
jewellery *n.* 68
job *n.* 107
join *v.*: Britain was joined to … 118
journey *n.* 119
juice *n.* 77
jump *v.* 17
jumper *n.* 77
jungle *n.* 15

K

keep *v.* 25
keep fit *v.* 25
Kenya *n.* 105
kept = p*ast of* 'keep' *v.* 79
Kilauea *n.* 58
kill *v.* 87
kinds (*n.*) of … 116
King, Martin Luther *n.* 79
knife *n.* (*pl.* knives) 39
know *v.* 33
know about *v.* 78

L

lake *n.* 58
Lake Tezcoco *n.* 81
land *v.* 21
land *n.* 116
landscape *n.* 58
large *adj.* 17
late *adj.* 75
later *adv.*: See you later. 53
lay *v.* 19
layer *n.* 138
leader *n.* 79
leaf *n.* (*pl.* leaves) 18
learn *v.* 20
leather *adj.* 67
leather *n.* 67
leave *v.* 21
left = *past of* 'leave' *v.* 92
leg *n.* 25
leisure *adj.*: leisure activities 98
leopard *n.* 17
lesson *n.* 38
Let's = let us *v.* 53
letter *n.* 34
level *n.* 25
life *n.* 19
lift *v.* 27
lift *n.* 124
light *n.* 19

light *adj.* 27
like *v.* 16
list *n.* 38
listen *v.* 20
live *v.* 16
local *adj.*: The local people … 107
locker *n.* 39
long *adj.* 50
Long Island *n.* 58
look like *v.* 50
lorry *n.* 110
lose *v.* 15
lost = *past of* 'lose' *v.* 15
lost *adj.*: We're lost. 114
loud *adj.* 32
loudly *adv.* 32
loudspeaker *n.* 38
lounge/dining room *n.* 139
love *v.*: I love it. 30
lucky *adj.* 73
lunch *n.* 38
lunchtime *n.*: at lunchtime 27
lung *n.* 25

M

machine *n.* 70
Machu Picchu *n.* 15
made = *past of* 'make' *v.* 68
magazine *n.* 25
main *adj.* 127
Maine *n.* 38
make *v.* 25
make somebody/something do something *v.* 25
make sure *v.* 87
making questions 18
mammal *n.* 10
manufacture *v.* 105
many *adj.* 10
map *n.* 58
market *n.* 81
Mathematics *n.* 39
Mauna Loa *n.* 58
meal *n.* 38
mean *v.* 33
meat *n.* 50
meat-eater *n.* 50
medal *n.*: gold medal 27
medicine *n.* 45
medium *adj.* 139
meet *v.* 53
melon *n.* 93
melt *v.* 65
memory *n.* 35
Mercury *n.* 15
message *n.* 76
metal *n.* 39
meteor *n.* 50
Mexico City *n.* 11

Middle East *n.* 85
milk *n.* 37
million 47
mind *v.*: I don't mind (doing …) 30
mine *n.* 16
Minnesota *n.* 58
miss *v.* 92
Mississippi River *n.* 58
modals 110
modern *adj.* 13
money *n.* 81
monsoon *n.* 85
monument *n.* 59
moon *n.* 11
morning *n.*: in the morning 51
Mount McKinley *n.* 58
mountain *n.* 58
mouth *n.* 14
move *v.* 25
'*much*' and '*many*' 95
multinational *n.* 107
muscle *n.* 25
museum *n.* 95
must *v.* 39
mystery *n.* 65

N

native *adj.* 78
nature *n.* 11
near *prep.* 15
nearby *adv.* 99
nearly *adv.* 87
need *v.* 24
neighbour *n.* 11
neutron *n.* 127
never *adv.* 73
New Orleans *n.* 58
New York *n.* 124
New Zealand *n.* 105
new *adj.* 10
news *n.* 90
newsagent's *n.* 113
next *adj.*: next week 91
next to *prep.* 114
nice *adj.* 16
night *n.*: at night 16
noise *n.* 46
noisy *adj.* 73
North America *n.* 45
North Vietnam *n.* 79
nothing *pron.* 45
now *adv.* 16
nowhere *adv.* 87
nuclear power *n.* 126
nurse *n.* 93

O

offer *v.* 99
Oh, bad luck! 73
old *adj.* 112
on the left of *prep.* 114
on the right of *prep.* 114

only *adj.* 14
opal *n.* 16
open *v.* 21
opposite *n.* 86
outdoor *adj.* 98
outside *n.* 46
over *adv.* 124
own *adj.* 107
oxygen *n.* 25

P

Pakistan *n.* 105
panic *n.* 124
paragraph *n.* 26
parents *n.* 99
parrot *n.* 10
partner *n.* 28
passenger *n.* 119
Past continuous 130
Past simple negatives 72
Past simple questions 72
Past simple: irregular verbs 71
Past simple: regular verbs 52
pasta *n.* 86
peace *n.* 37
perhaps *adv.* 20
person *n.* 26
Peru *n.* 15
petrol *n.* 88
pie *n.* 93
piece *n.* 10
pig *n.* 70
place *n.* 45
plane *n.* 64
planet *n.* 10
Plans: going to 91
plant *n.* 45
plant *v.* 45
plant-eater *n.* 50
play (*v.*) football 10
play (*v.*) the piano 10
pledge *n.* 38
plug *n.* 128
Pluto *n.* 15
poem *n.* 57
polar *adj.* 85
police *n.* 65
police officer *n.* 93
pollen *n.* 14
popular *adj.* 25
Portland *n.* 38
possible *adj.* 17
post office *n.* 113
pot *n.* 70
power station *n.* 126
powerful *adj.* 20
practise *v.* 28
praying mantids *n. pl.* (*sing.* mantis) 11
prehistoric *n.* 52
Present continuous 15
Present simple 13

Present simple questions 14
present *n.* 75
primary products *n.* 104
printing press *n.* 64
prison *n.* 124
prisoner *n.* 124
probably *adv.* 17
produce *v.* 79
pronounce *v.* 12
pronouns 14
protein *n.* 37
proton *n.* 127
put *v.* 73
put = *past of* 'put' *v.* 73
put down *v.* 119
put up *v.* 119
puzzle *n.* 10

Q

question *n.* 30
quick *adj.* 32
quickly *adv.* 25
quiet *adj.* 32
quietly *adv.* 31
quiz n. (*pl.* quizzes) 39

R

raft *n.* 99
rain *n.* 11
rainforest *n.* 44
rainy *adj.* 14
rat *n.* 119
raw *adj.* 85
raw materials *n.* 104
reacting 75
read *v.* 34
really *adv.*: No, not really. 73
receive *v.* 87
record *n.* 55
reduce *v.* 126
reflect *v.* 85
region *n.* 86
regular and irregular verbs: Past simple 115
religious *adj.* 78
remember *v.* 134
repair *v.* 124
repeat *v.* 34
repel *v.* 127
reporter *n.* 28
representative *n.* 90
reptile *n.* 19
restaurant *n.* 16
result *n.* 118
rice *n.* 45
rise *v.* 10
river *n.* 58
road *n.* 16
rock climbing *n.* 98
rocket *n.* 21
Rocky Mountains *n.* 58
root *n.* 46
rose = *past of* 'rise' *v.* 87

Wordlist/Index **159**

round-the-world *adj.* 64
rubber (plant) *n.* 45
rule *n.* 39
run *v.* 39
running *n.* 24

S

same *adj.* 39
sandstorm *n.* 65
sandwich *n.* 111
sandy *adj.* 58
save *v.* 119
saw = *past of* 'see' *v.* 66
school *n.* 16
Science *n.* 39
scientist *n.* 20
scream *v.* 130
sea *n.* 87
search *v.* 20
season *n.* 88
seatbelt *n.* 65
see *v.* 59
See you later. 53
sell *v.* 70
send *v.* 18
sentence *n.* 21
separate *adj.* 48
settler *n.* 79
shape poems *n.* 57
sheep *n.* (*pl.* sheep) 67
ship *n.* 64
shoe *n.* 105
shop *n.* 16
Shop *n.* 39
shop assistant *n.* 93
short *adj.* 26
shorts *n.* 77
shout *v.* 39
Siberia *n.* 17
sign *n.* 20
signal *n.* 20
silly *adj.* 82
singer *n.* 32
Sioux *n.* 79
sister *n.* 72
size *n.* 13
skeleton *n.* 59
skin *n.* 17
sky *n.* 19
slave *n.* 78
slavery *n.* 78
sleep *v.* 14
slept = *past of* 'sleep' *v.* 124
slow *adj.* 32
slowly *adv.* 31
small *adj.* 17
smoke *v.* 39
snack *n.* 104
snake *n.* 57
snow *n.* 65
so *conj.* 81
socket *n.* 128
sold = *past of* 'sell' *v.* 81
solitary *adj.* 17
'some' and 'any' 35
sometimes *adv.* 70
song *n.* 12
south *n.* 18
South America *n.* 45
South Vietnam *n.* 79
South East Asia *n.* 45
space *n.* 20
spaceship *n.* 19
Spain *n.* 90
Spanish *n.* 11
speak *v.* 11
speciality *n.* 116
spectacular *adj.* 58
speech *n.* 79
speed *n.* 119
spell *v.* 12
spelling 31
spend *v.* (time) 17
spend *v.* (money) 138
spider *n.* 19
spoke = *past of* 'speak' *v.* 71
sports centre *n.* 16
sport *n.* 24
spot *n.* 17
spring *n.* 116
square *n.* 81
squash *n.* 24
stamp *n.* 113
star *n.* 20
start *v.* 20
stay *v.* 70
steam *n.* 126
still *adv.* 27
strange *adj.* 19
stranger *n.* 70
street *n.* 81
strong *adj.* 11
student *n.* 38
subject *n.* 39
subway *n.* *AmE* (*BrE* underground) 124
suddenly *adv.* 25
sugar *n.* 78
suggesting and inviting 55
suitcase *n.* 111
summer *n.* 116
sun *n.* 15
sunglasses *n.* 77
sunny *adj.* 16
supermarket *n.* 113
surface *n.* 45
sweater *n.* 73
sweet *adj.* 32
sweet *n.* 72
swimming *n.* 24

T

T-shirt *n.* 77
table tennis *n.* 24
tail *n.* 50
take *v.* 25
Take the second turning ... 133
take (time) *v.* 119
talk *v.* 21
tall *adj.* 13
tank *n.* 88
Tanzania *n.* 105
tarantula *n.* 10
tax *n.* 78
taxi driver *n.* 93
tea *n.* 78
teacher *n.* 38
team *n.* 26
technology *n.* 107
telephone *n.* 16
telescope *n.* 20
tell *v.* 53
temperate *adj.* 85
test *n.* 34
That's terrible! 73
the future 91
The Netherlands *n.* 87
The Sahel *n.* 87
these *pron. pl.* (*sing.* this) 13
thick *adj.* 50
thin *adj.* 50
thing *n.* 16
think *v.* 15
thought = *past of* 'think' *v.* 15
thousand: thousands of people 16
threw = *past of* 'throw' *v.* 78
throw *v.* 78
ticket *n.* 53
tidy *adj.* 39
timetable *n.* 27
to be afraid *v.* 57
today *adv.* 59
tomorrow *adv.* 91
tonight *adv.* 91
too *adv.*: too far 18
too little *adv.* 37
too much *adv.* 37
took = *past of* 'take' *v.* 81
tool *n.* 64
tooth *n.* (*pl.* teeth) 50
toothpaste *n.* 113
touch *v.* 133
tourist *n.* 59
tourist information office *n.* 133
town *n.* 16
track *n.* 119
traditional *adj.* 85
traffic *n.* 17
traffic lights *n.* 133
train *v.* 27
train station *n.* 113
training *n.* 30
transformer *n.* 126
transport *n.* 81
travel *v.* 70
tree *n.* 16
tribe *n.* 79
trip *n.* 75
tropical *adj.* 86
trouble *n.* 124
true *adj.* 46
tunnel *n.* 118
turn *v.* 126
Turn left. 133
Turn right. 133
type *n.* 10
tyre *n.* 105

U

ugly *adj.* 14
under *prep.* 57
underground *n.* 119
underground *adj.* 16
understand *v.* 32
unfortunately *adv.* 45
uniform *n.* 93
United Kingdom *n.* 90
United States of America *n.* 20
universe *n.* 20
USA *see* United States of America 50
use *v.* 68
useful *adj.* 12
usually *adv.* 14
Utah *n.* 59

V

valley *n.* 52
vapour *n.* 46
vegetables *n.* 37
verb + '-ing' 30
village *n.* 70
visit *v.* 52
vitamin *n.* 37
volcano *n.* 58
volt *n.* 126

W

wage *n.* 107
wait *v.* 17
walking *n.* 24
wall *n.* 87
want *v.* 33
war *n.* 78
warm *adj.* 86
warning *n.* 88
'was' and 'were' = *past of* 'be' 51
watch out *v.* 59
water *n.* 16
water vapour *n.* 46
way *n.* 25
weak *adj.* 16
weapon *n.* 39
wear *v.* 85
weather *n.* 45
weekend *n.* 73
weights *n.* 27
well *adv.* 32
went = *past of* 'go' *v.* 10
west *n.* 58
wet *adj.* 45
whale *n.* 18
What about ...?: What about school? 30
What does ... mean? 12
What time is it? 13
wheat *n.* 104
Why don't (we) ...? 54
wide *adj.* 59
win *v.* 27
wind *n.* 87
window cleaner *n.* 93
windy *adj.* 16
wing *n.* 19
winter *n.* 18
wire *n.* 105
Wollemi Pines *n.* 47
won = *past of* 'win' *v.* 79
wonder *n.* 59
wonder *v.* 114
wood *n.* 39
wooden *adj.* 86
wool *n.* 68
word *n.* 26
wore = *past of* 'wear' *v.* 68
work *v.* 16
world *n.* 18
'would': making an offer 111
write *v.* 21
writing *n.* 81
wrote = *past of* 'write' *v.* 78

Y

year *n.* 15
Yellowstone National Park *n.* 59
yesterday *adv.* 72
YHA *see* Youth Hostels Association 99
yoghurt *n.* 68
You lucky thing! 73
young *adj.* 99
Youth Hostels Association *n.* 99

Z

zebra *n.* 17
zoo *n.* 75